Pac
Templa

Edited by Ju Hai

GINGKO PRESS

First Published by Gingko Press in the United States of America in 2009
by arrangement with Liaoning Science and Technology Publishing House

First   Edition
Gingko Press, Inc.
1321 Fifth Street
Berkeley, CA 94710, USA

Phone (510) 898 1195
Fax (510) 898 1195
www.gingkopress.com

ISBN: 978-1-58423-337-4

Editor: Ju Hai
Layout Designer: Ju Hai
Cover Designer:

Printed in China

Contents

Introduction

Packaging always performs an essential function in the marketing field. On many occasions, it is the packaging structure, rather than the product itself, that catches the consumers' eye.

In some cases, consumers can easily identify the product from dinstinctive packaging structure; in other cases, manufacturers use unique packaging structure to make the products more attractive. At the same time, packaging structure also has its practical function —to protect product from being damaged in transporting.

A number of primary elements should be considered in designing any packaging structure: the size, the material, the depth of the material, and the technology. In addition, whether these elements are all suitable for the product is also of great concern.

Packaging Templates is an invaluable reference book for people engaged in the packaging industry. Each structure presented in this book consists of a template and a final product.

About the CD-ROM

The template for each design can be found on the accompanying CD-ROM. While the designs can be used to develop new packaging solutions, the images themselves cannot be used for any type of commercial use without the permission of the publishers. The CD can be used on most operating systems.

International standards

A.L = Length of Box

B.W = Width of Box

C.D = Depth of Box

Terms

R.T.E.	Reverse Tuck End
S.T.E.	Straight Tuck End (For window box)
French R.T.E.	French Reverse Tuck End (For cosmetics)
Auto Bottom	Auto Assemble
123Bottom	Snap Lock Bottom (For cosmetics,wine and food)
Six/Four-points-glued Box	Beer Tray

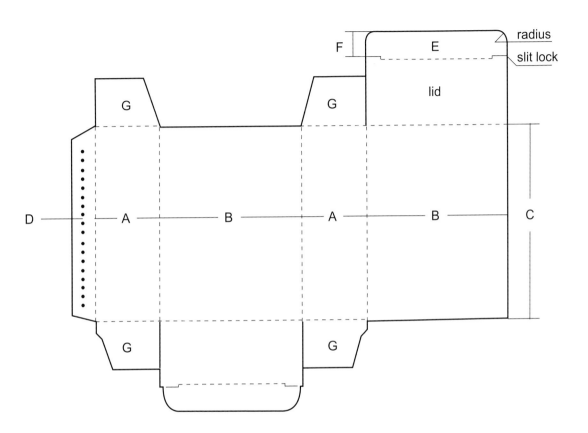

radius

slit lock

F E

lid

G G

D A B A B C

G G

007

A. L=Length   E. Tuck
B. W=Width   F. Shoulder
C. D=Depth   G. Dust flap
D. Glue flap

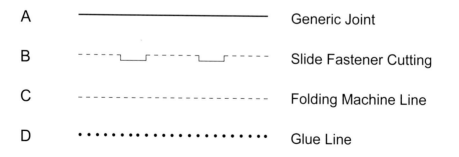

B=thickness
R=radius

(A)

R

1/2B — shoulder

5mm

B

15°

1/2W+1/2tuck
45°

shoulder

W

L

B

B

W

(B)

R

tuck

15°

shoulder

1/2W+1/2tuck

W

L

B

W

008

A	———————————	Generic Joint
B	– – – ⌐_⌐ – – ⌐_⌐ – – –	Slide Fastener Cutting
C	– – – – – – – – – – – – –	Folding Machine Line
D	• • • • • • • • • • • • •	Glue Line

Locking Methods

1. Auto Locks
2. Top panel Locks
3. Side and End Panel Locks
4. Click Locks
5. Foot Locks
6. Double Locks
7. Gusseted Dust Locks
8. Dust Flap Locks
9. Butterfly Locks
10. Floral Locks

Auto Locks

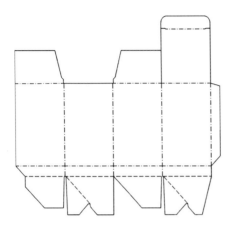

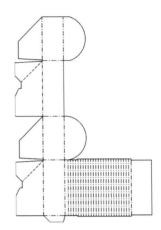

010

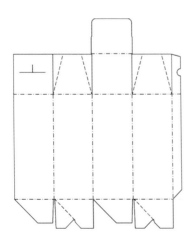

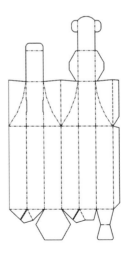

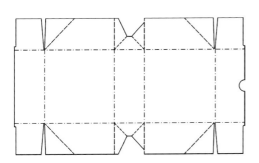

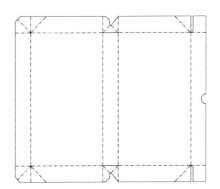

011

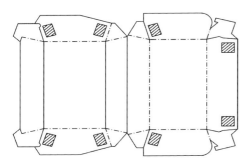

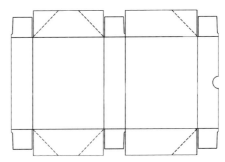

Side and End Panel Locks

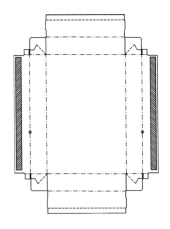

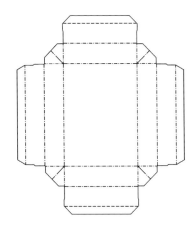

012

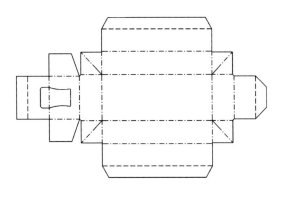

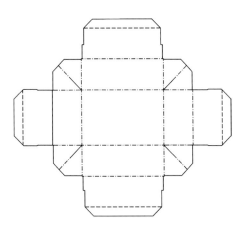

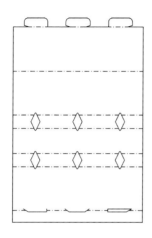

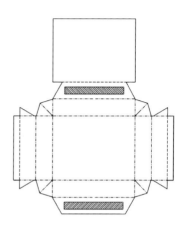

013

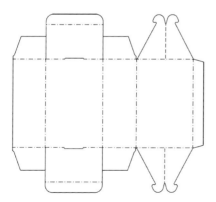

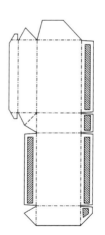

Foot Locks

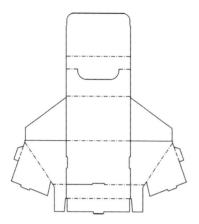

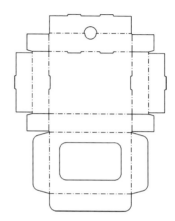

014

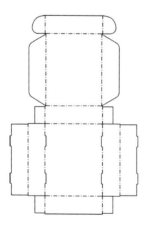

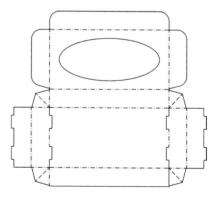

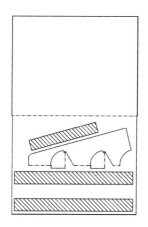

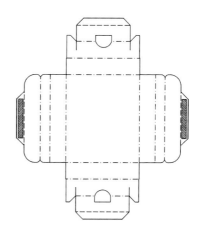

015

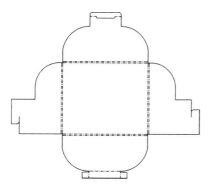

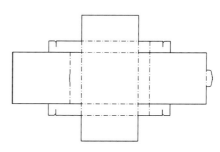

Gusseted Dust Locks

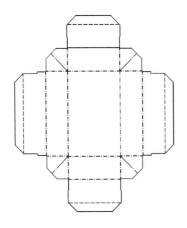

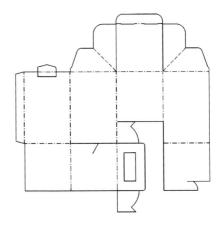

016

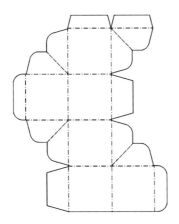

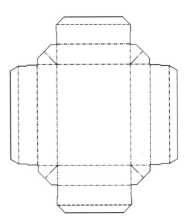

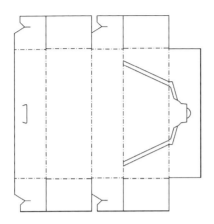

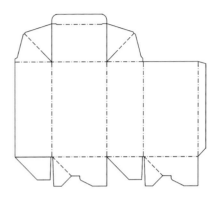

017

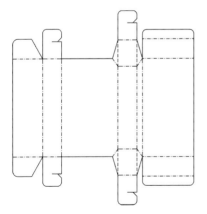

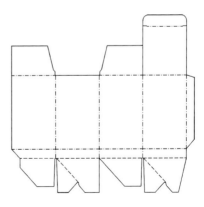

Butterfly Locks

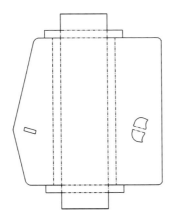

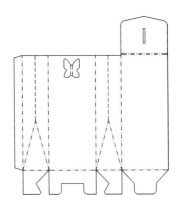

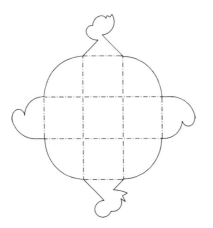

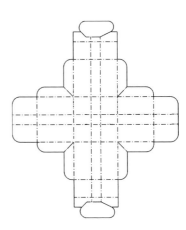

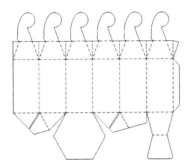

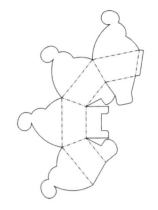

019

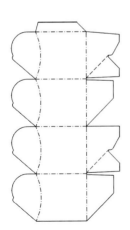

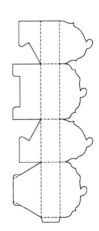

Basic Structures

1. Universal
2. Holder
3. Dispenser
4. Divider
5. Combination
6. Carrier
7. Window Carton
8. Display Box
9. Display Rack
10. Book-shaped
11. House-shaped
12. Diamond
13. Column Box
14. Triangular
15. Trapezoidal Box
16. Pentagram
17. Hanging Box
18. Italic
19. Lining
20. Special
21. Hollow Wall Tray
22. Double Side Wall
23. Auto Bottom
24. Tray
25. Sealed Ends
26. Tapered Top
27. Roof Top
28. Polygonal Top
29. Floral Top
30. Hinged Lid
31. Flip Top
32. Dome Top
33. Perforated Flip Top
34. Frame-shaped

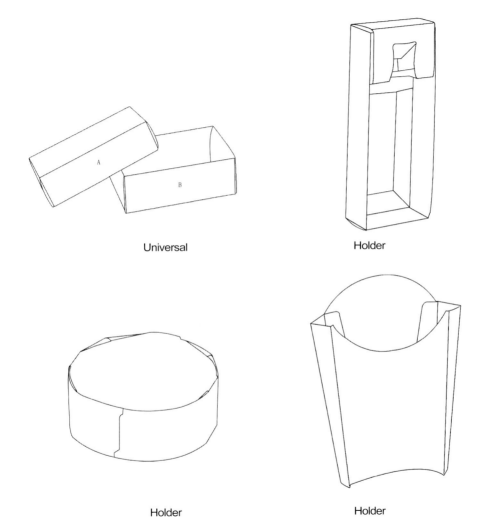

Universal

Holder

Holder

Holder

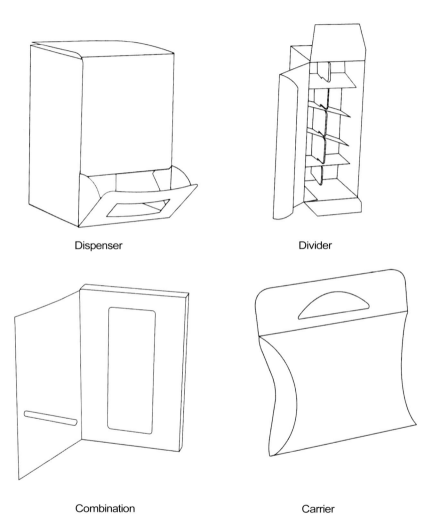

Dispenser

Divider

Combination

Carrier

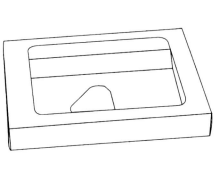

Window Carton

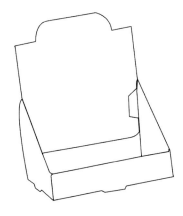

Display Box

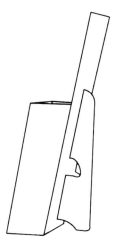

Display Rack

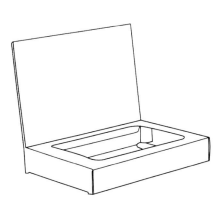

Book-shaped

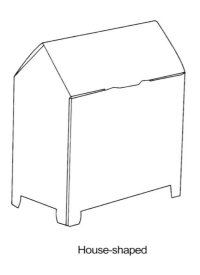

House-shaped

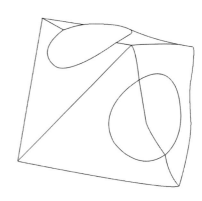

Diamond

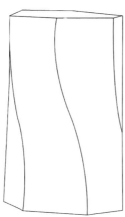

Columnar Box

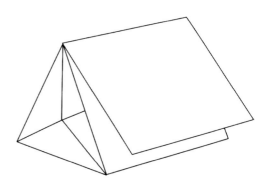

Triangular

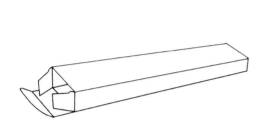

Trapezoidal Box

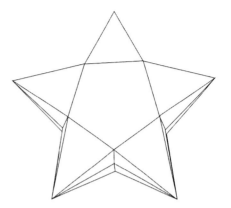

Diamond

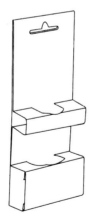

Hanging Box

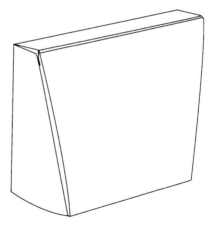

Italic

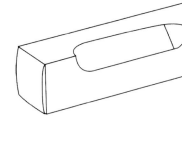

Lining

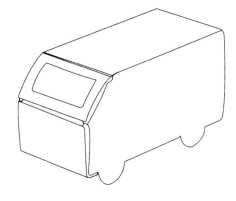

Special

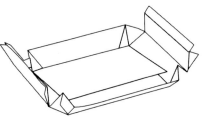

Hollow Wall Tray

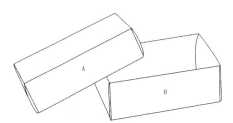

Double Side Wall

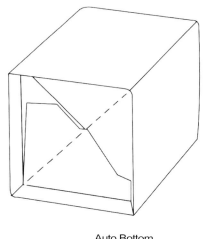

Auto Bottom

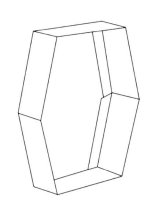

Tray

Sealed Ends

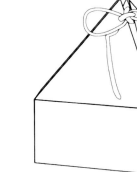

Tapered Top

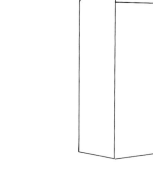

Roof Top

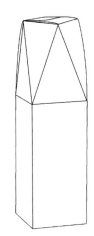

Polygonal Top

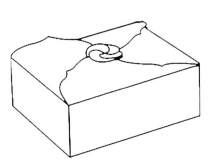

Floral Top

Hinged Lid

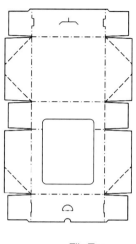

Flip Top

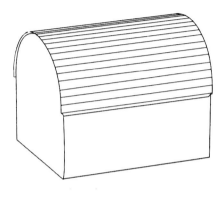

Dome Top

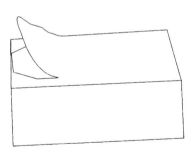

Perforated Flip Top

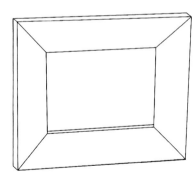

Frame-shaped

Hanging Boxes

032   Candle Box

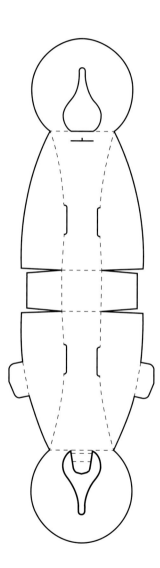

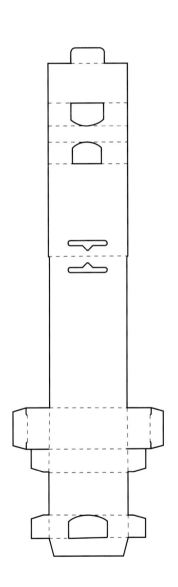

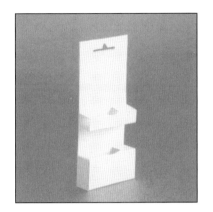

Hanging Box 033

034 **Box with Hanging Panel**

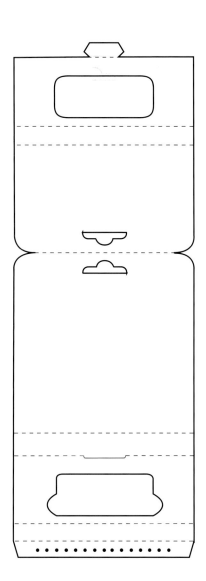

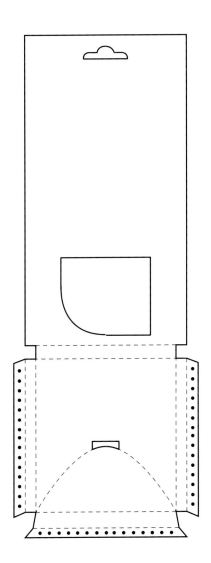

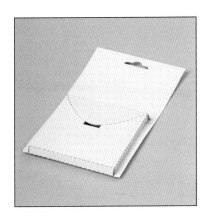

Box with Hanging Panel   035

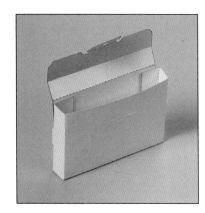

036 Tuck Lock with Hanging Hole

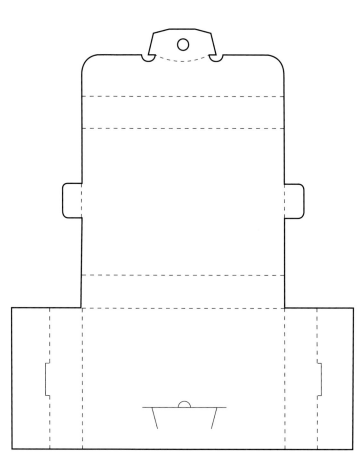

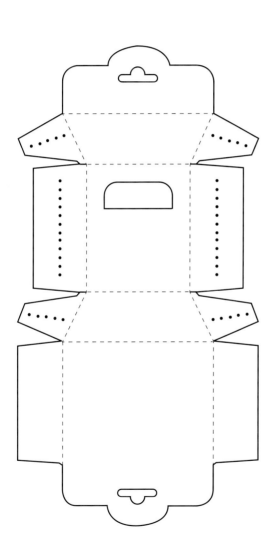

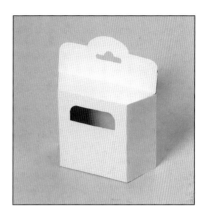

Hanging Panel and Window 037

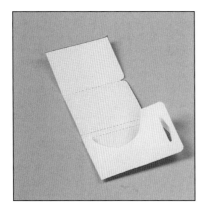

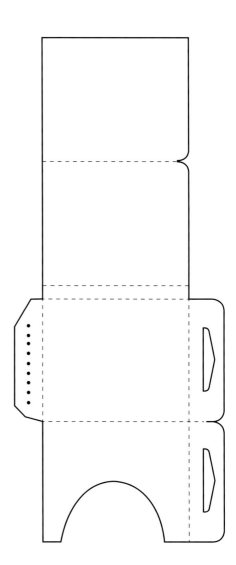

038 **Hanging Folder**

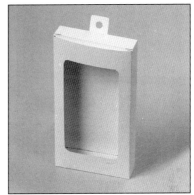

Hanging Tab 039

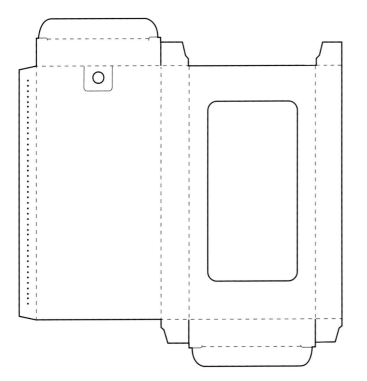

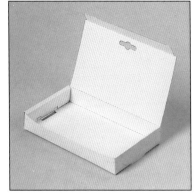

040   Hanging Hole

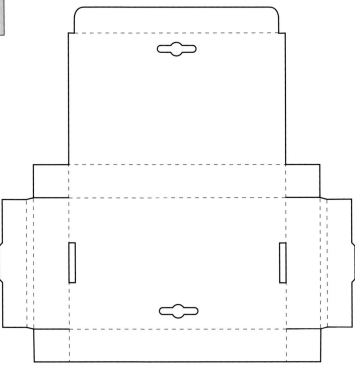

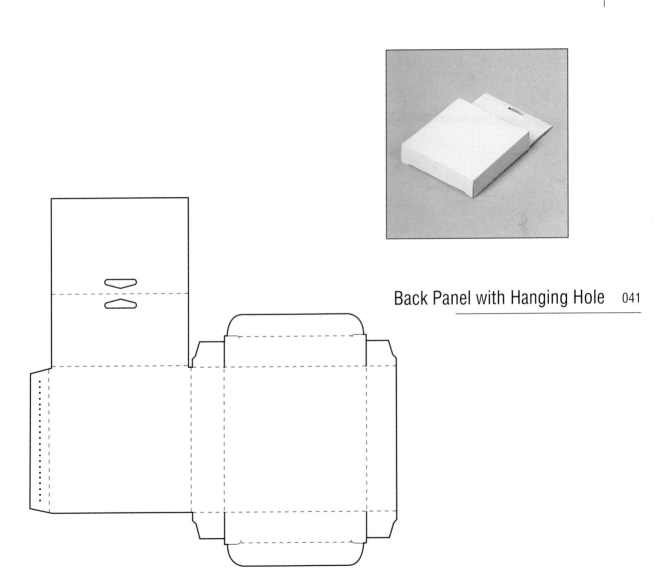

Back Panel with Hanging Hole   041

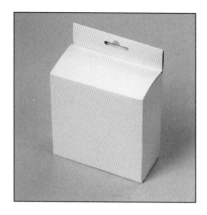

042 **Back Panel with Hanging Hole**

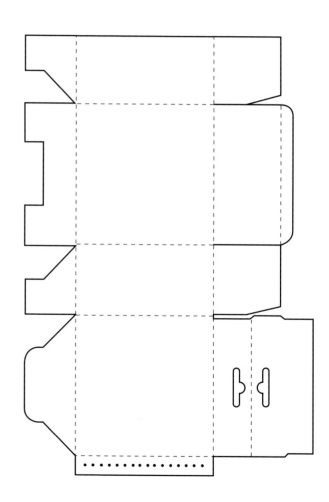

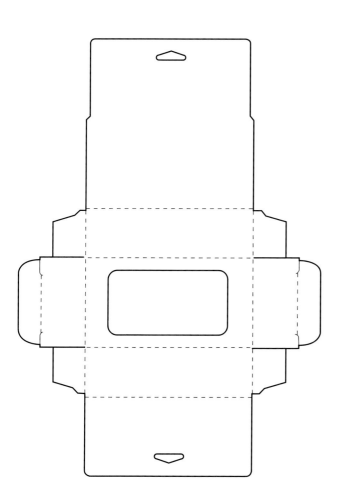

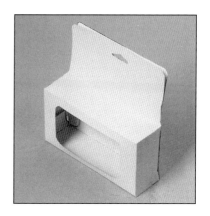

Back Panel with Hanging Hole   043

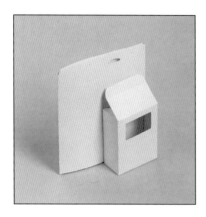

044 **Box with Hanging Panel**

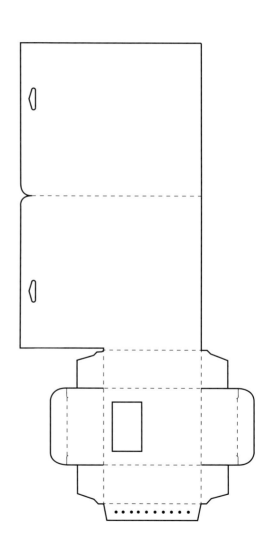

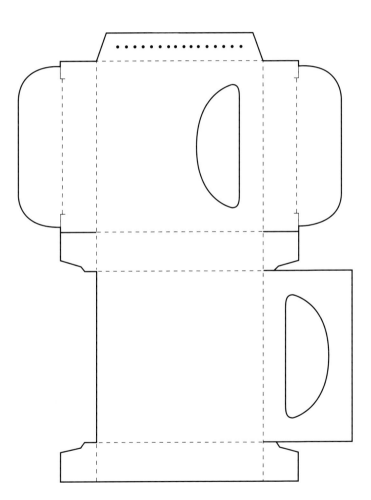

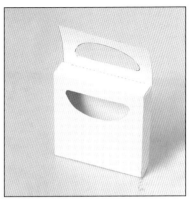

Hanging Panel and Window   045

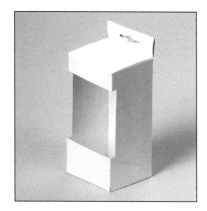

046   Hanging Panel and Window

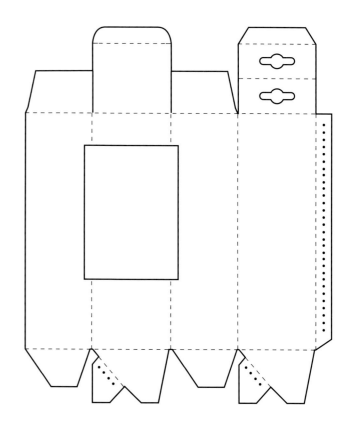

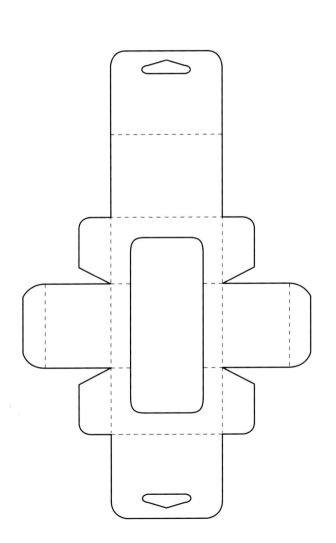

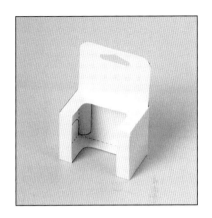

Hanging Panel and Window 047

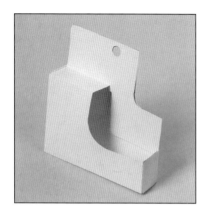

048   Hanging Display Panel

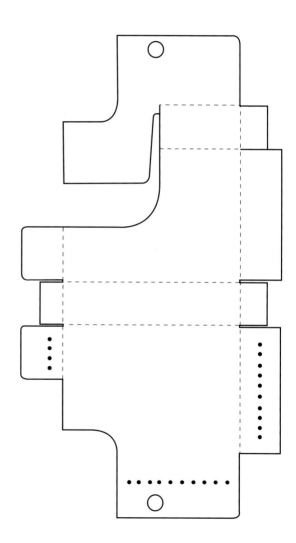

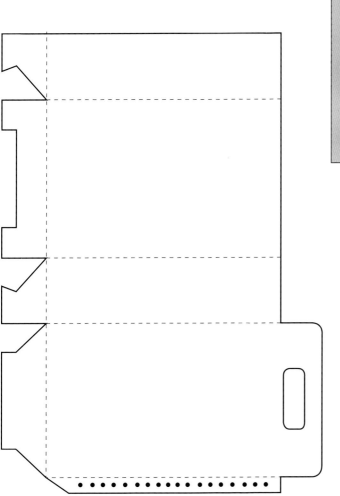

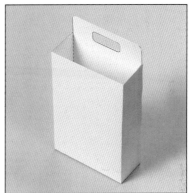

Hanging Display Box   049

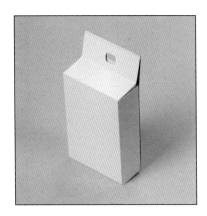

050 Hanging Display Box

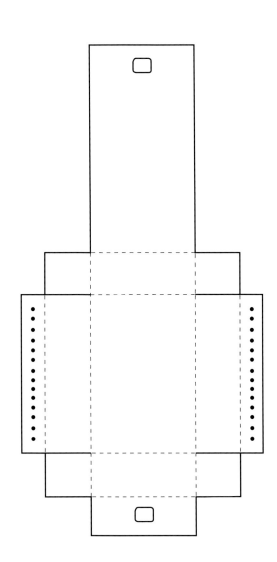

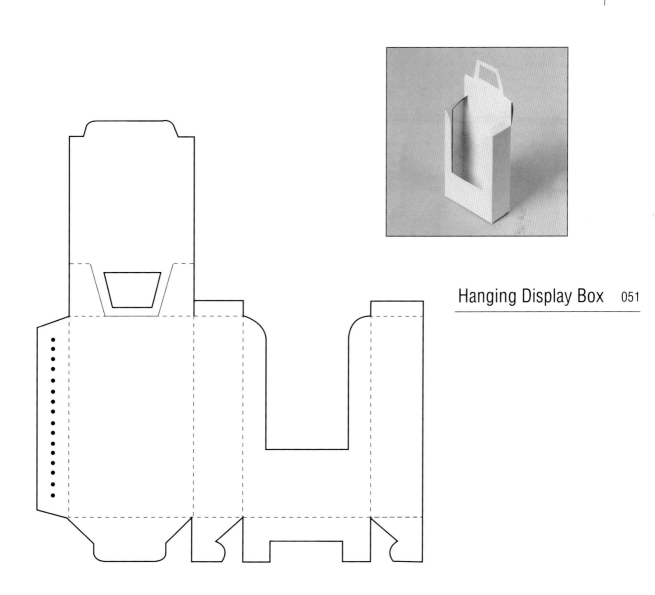

Hanging Display Box   051

Presentation Boxes

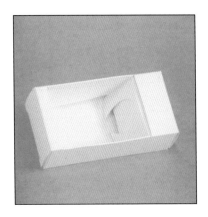

054 Auto Wrapping Machine Box

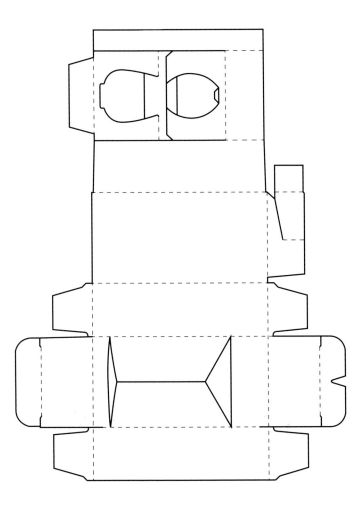

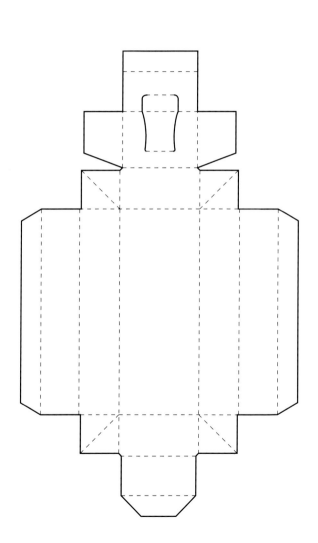

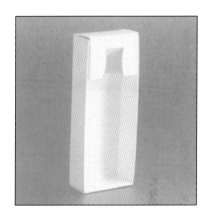

Bottle Box 055

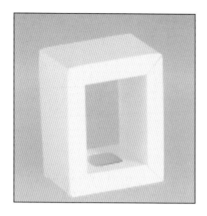

056 Frame-shaped Perfume Box

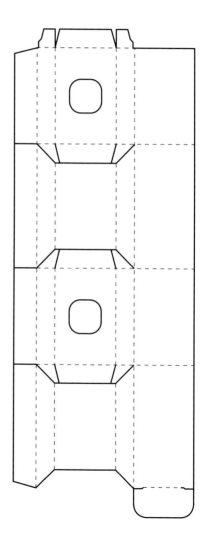

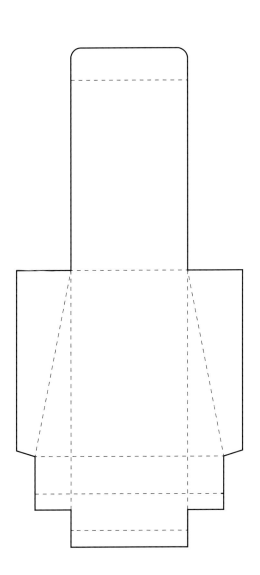

Business Card Display Box 057

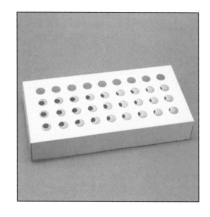

058 Lollipops Display Box

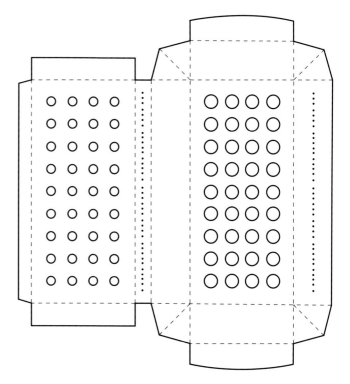

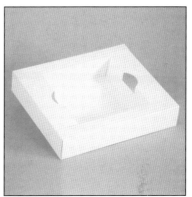

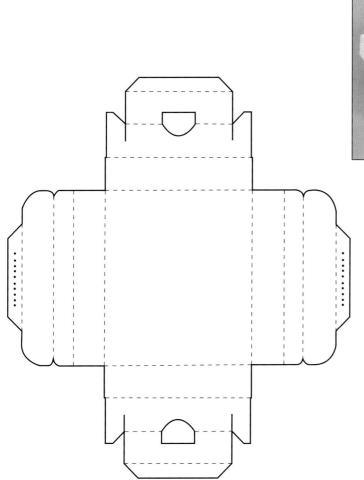

Frame-shaped Box   059

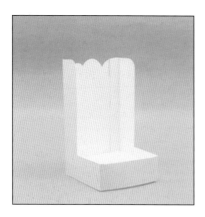

060 Candle Display Box

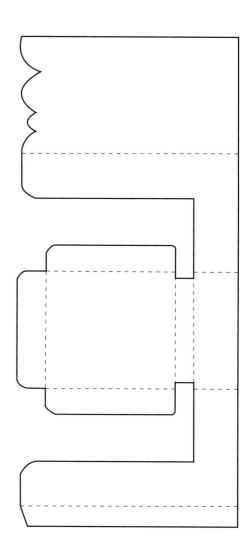

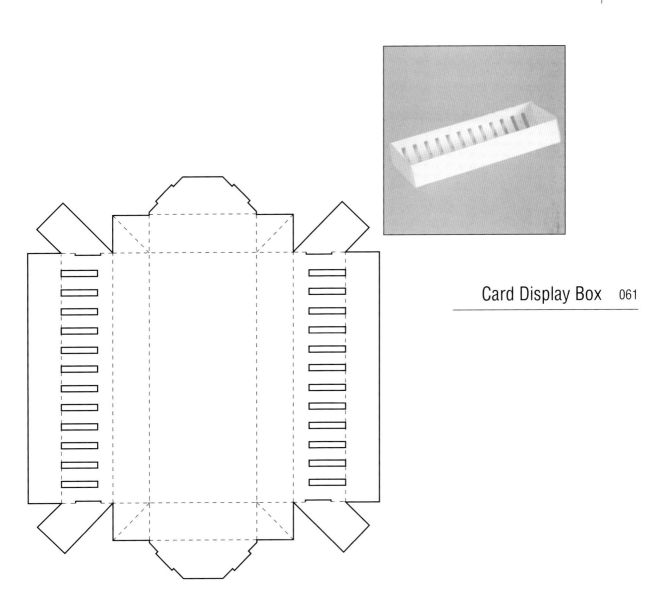

Card Display Box 061

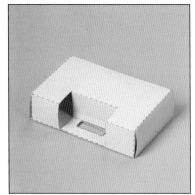

062 Hanging Display Box

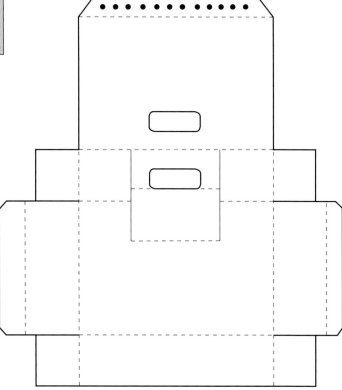

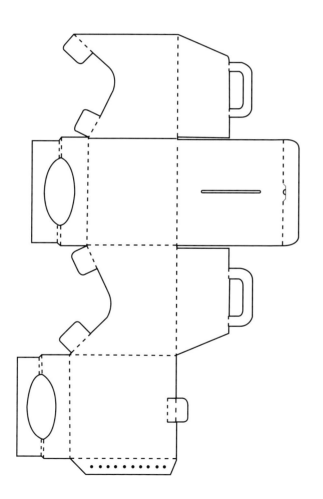

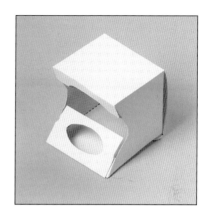

Exhibiting Display Box 063

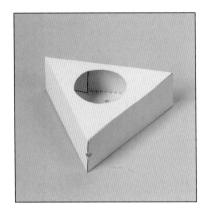

064 Exhibiting Display Box

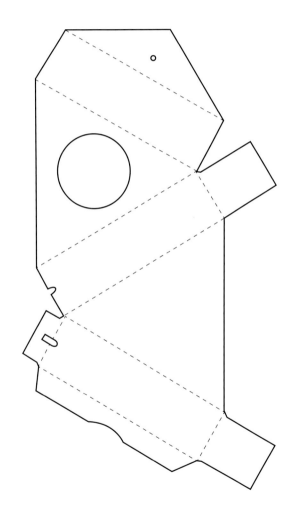

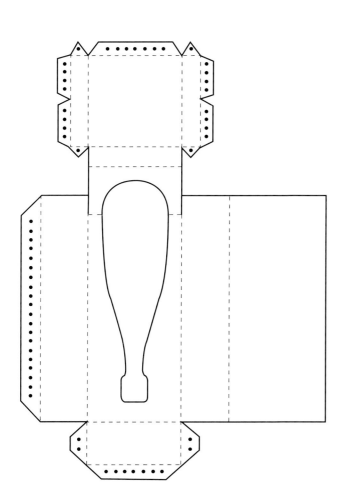

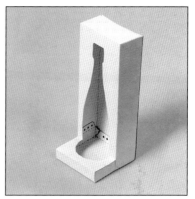

Exhibiting Display Box 065

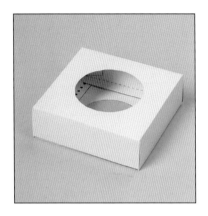

066   Exhibiting Display Box

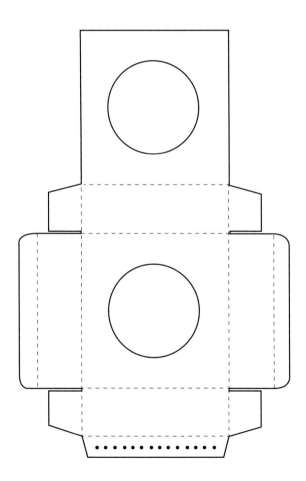

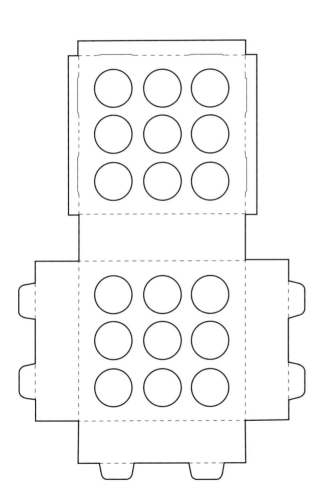

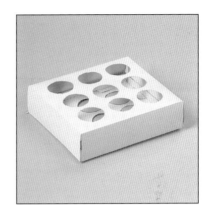

Exhibiting Display Box 067

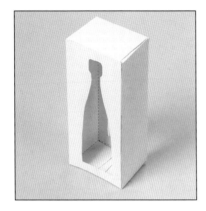

068 Exhibiting Display Box

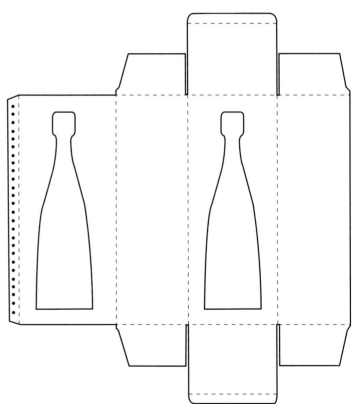

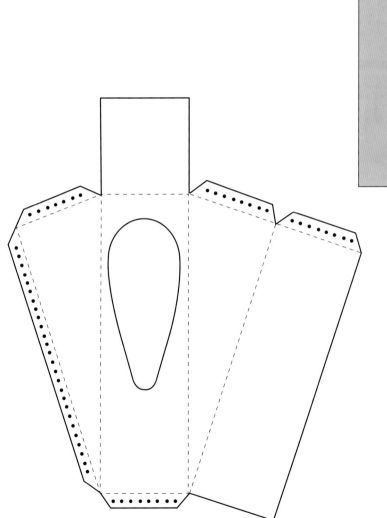

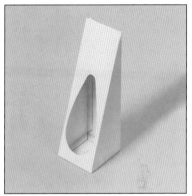

Exhibiting Display Box 069

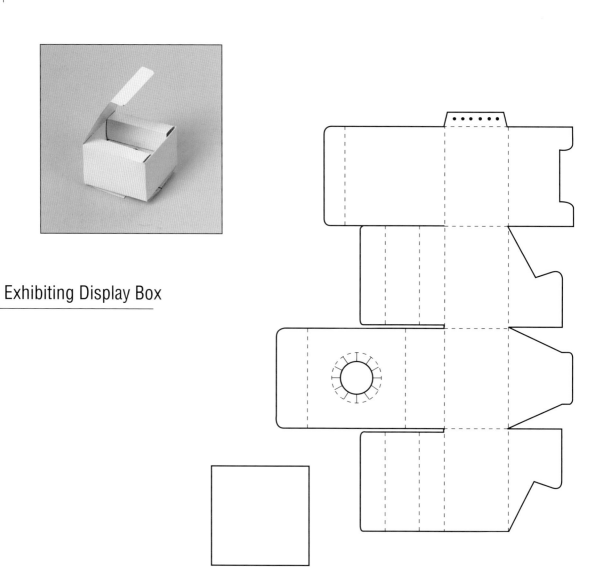

070 Exhibiting Display Box

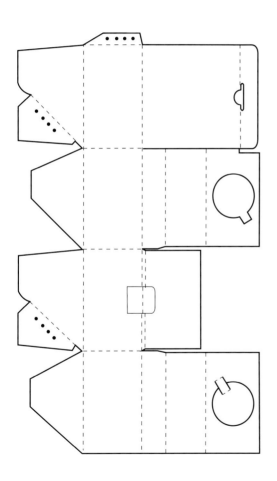

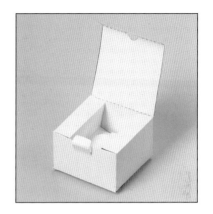

Exhibiting Display Box 071

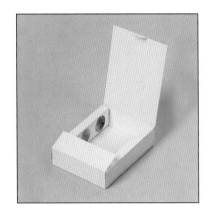

072 Exhibiting Display Box

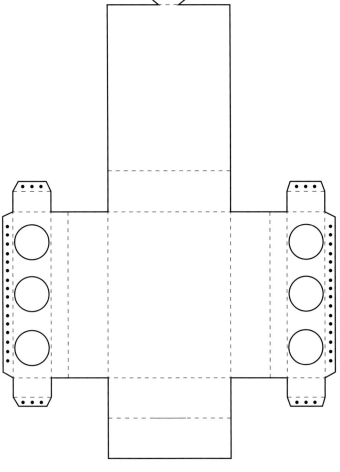

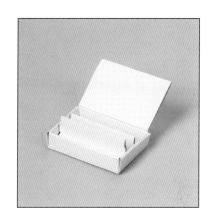

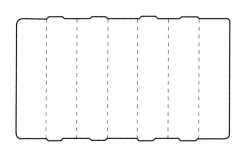

Exhibiting Display Box 073

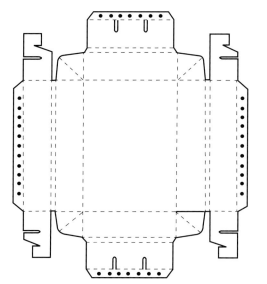

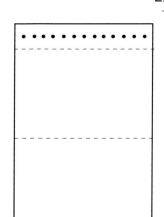

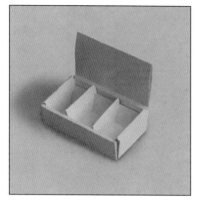

074 Exhibiting Display Box

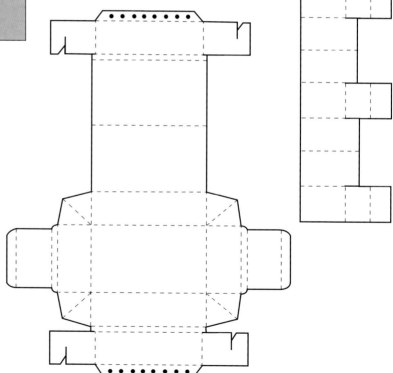

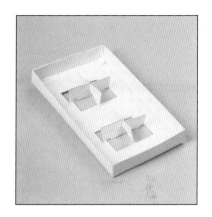

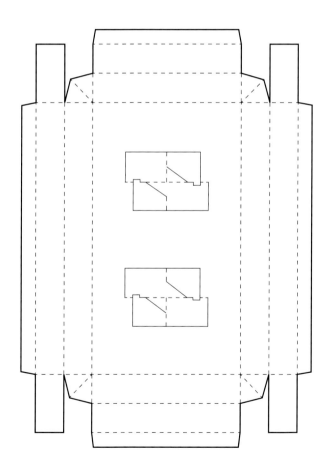

Exhibiting Display Box 075

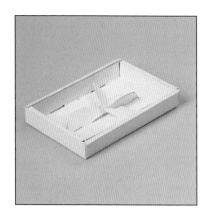

Exhibiting Display Box

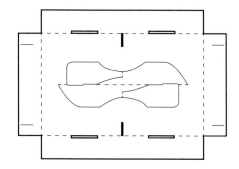

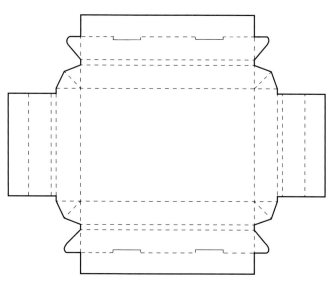

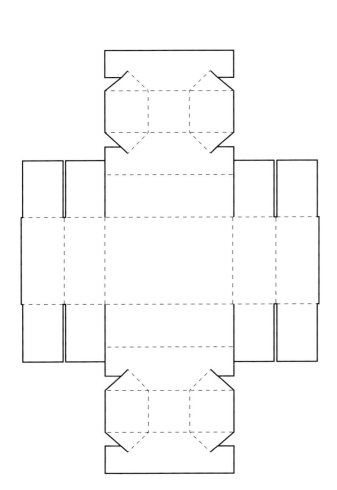

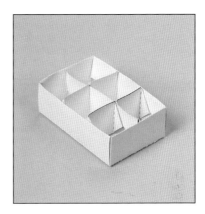

Exhibiting Display Box   077

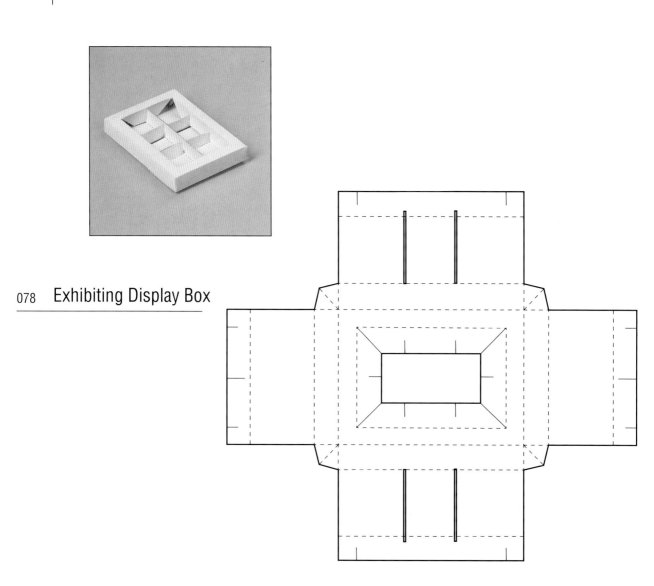

078   Exhibiting Display Box

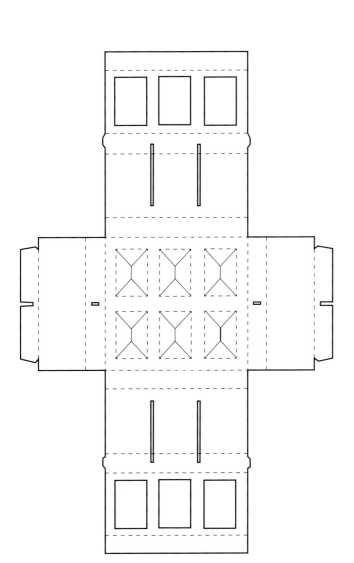

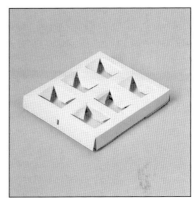

Exhibiting Display Box 079

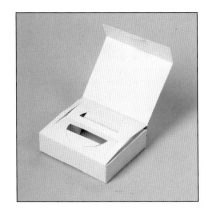

080   **Exhibiting Display Box**

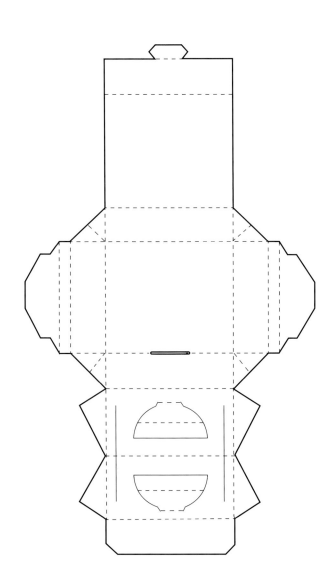

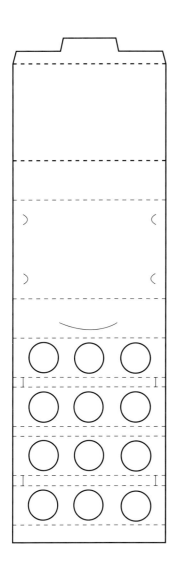

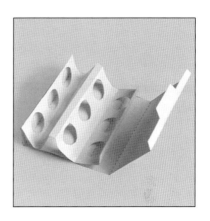

Exhibiting Display Box   081

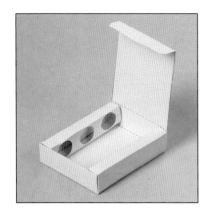

082 Exhibiting Display Box

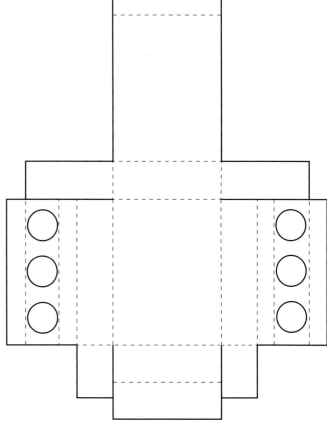

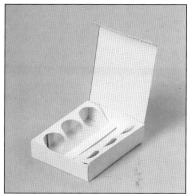

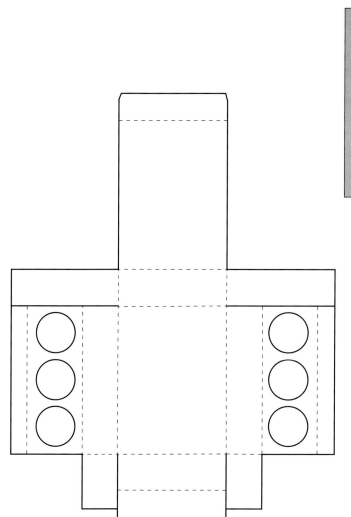

Exhibiting Display Box 083

084 Exhibiting Display Box

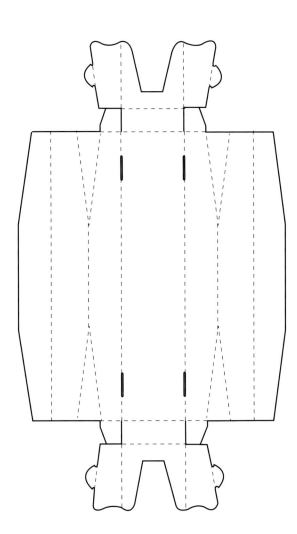

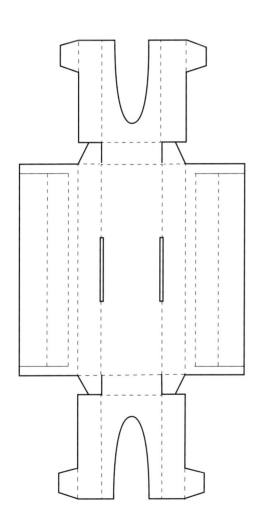

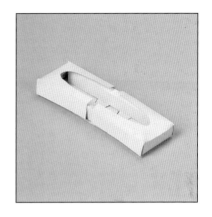

Exhibiting Display Box   085

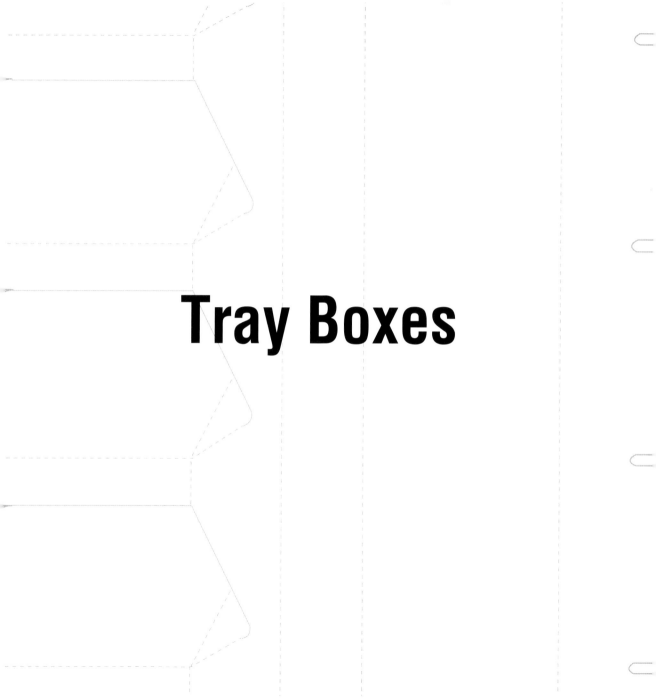

Tray Boxes

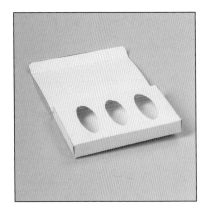

088 Exhibiting Display Box

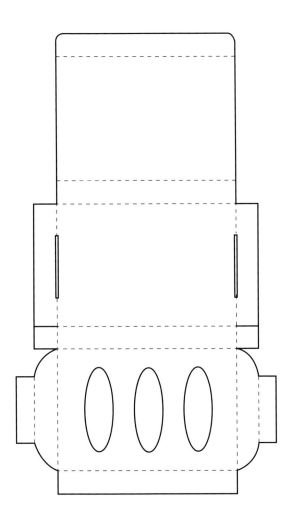

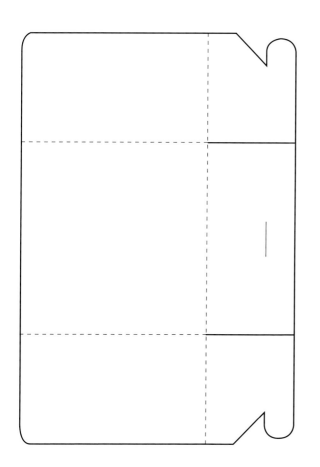

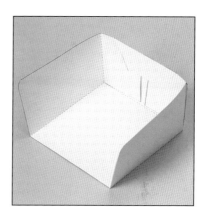

Open Ended Tray   089

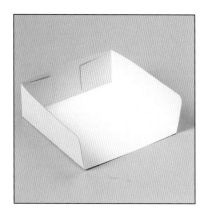

090   Open Ended Tray

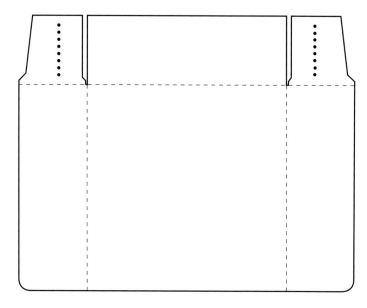

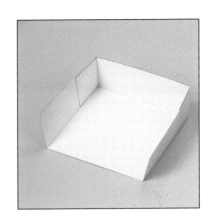

Open Ended Tray 091

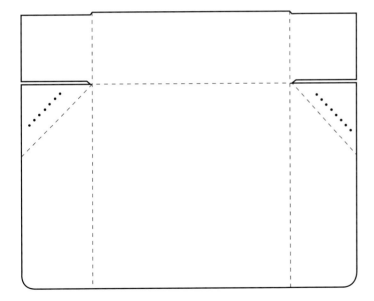

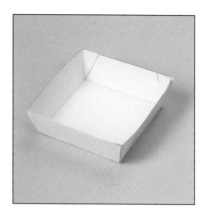

092   Tapered Tray

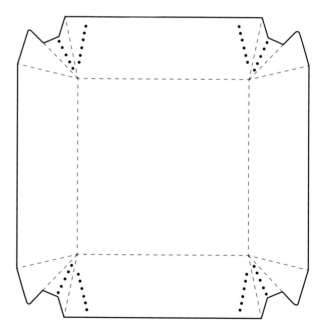

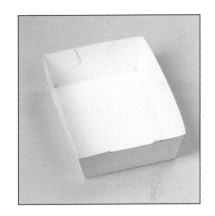

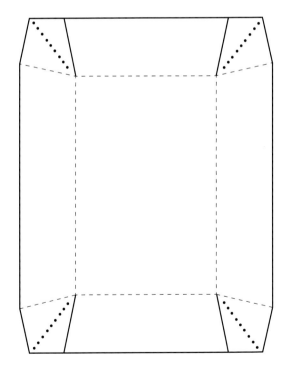

Tapered Tray 093

094   Tapered Tray

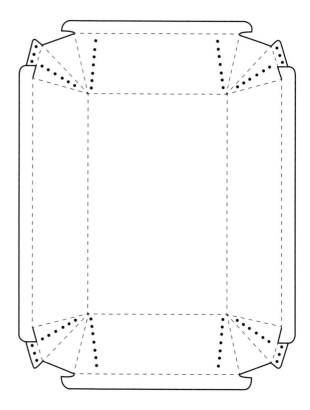

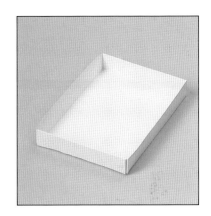

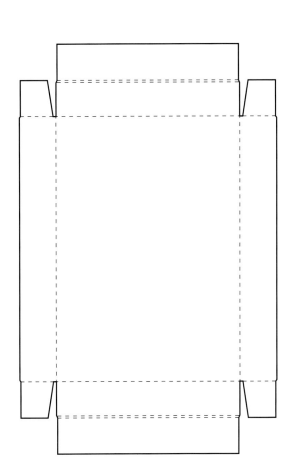

Display Tray   095

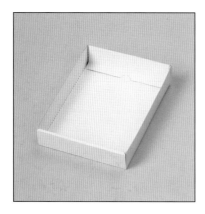

096   Tray with Tuck-in Side Panels

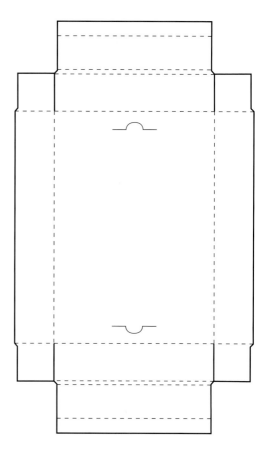

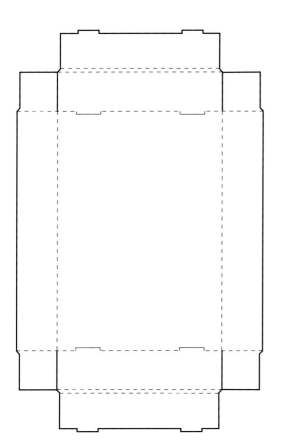

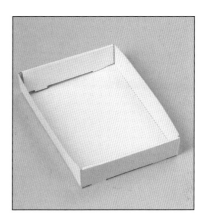

Tray with Tuck-in Side Panels 097

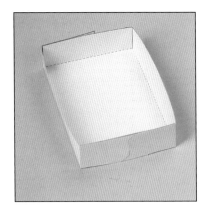

098   Tray with Side Panel Locks

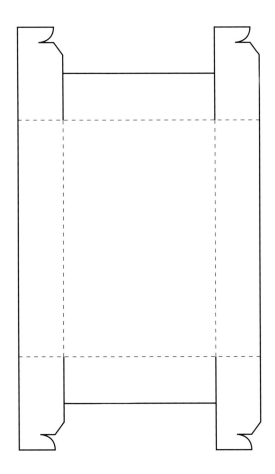

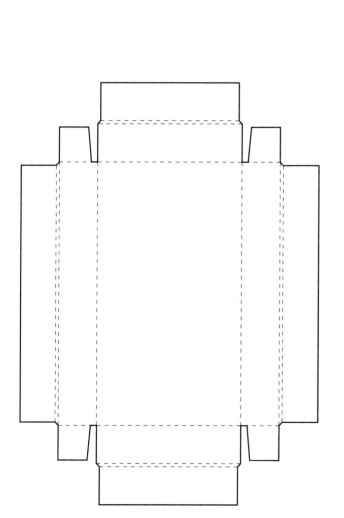

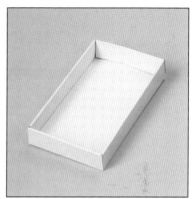

Double Wall Tray   099

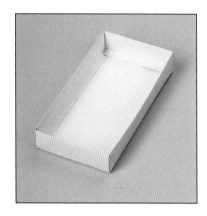

Double Wall Tray

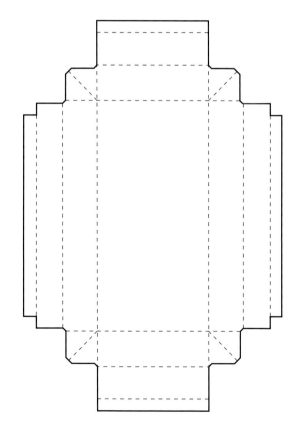

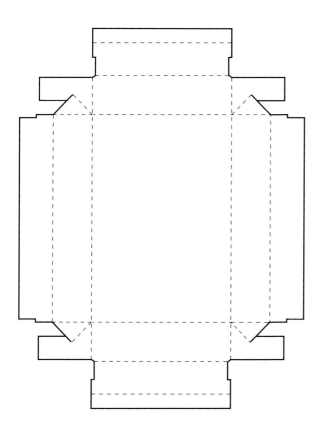

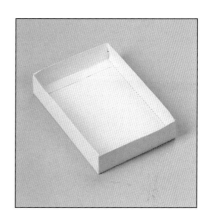

Double Wall Tray 101

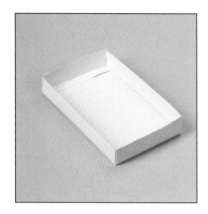

Double Wall Tray

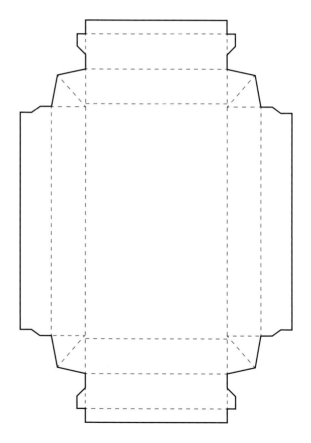

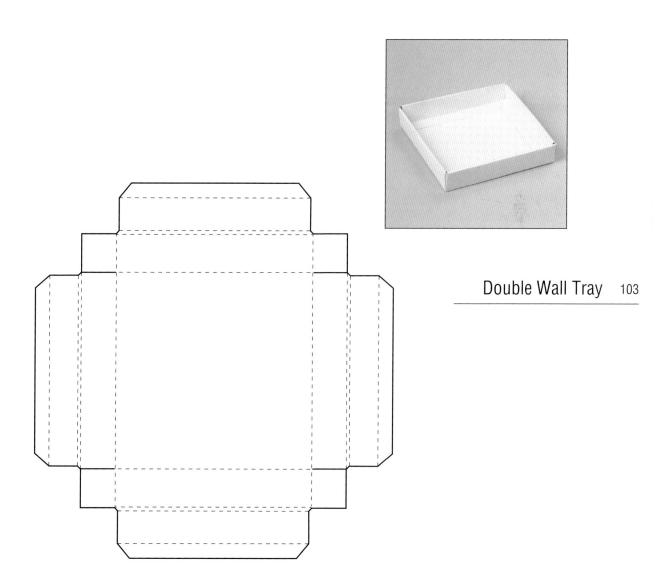

Double Wall Tray 103

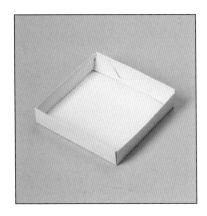

Double Wall Tray with Side Panel Lock

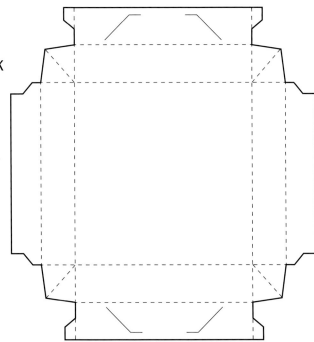

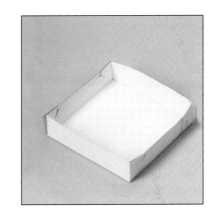

Tray with Side Panel Locks 105

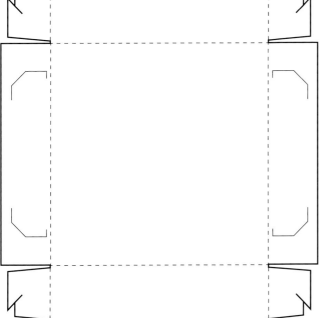

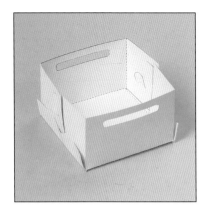

Tray with Side Panel Locks

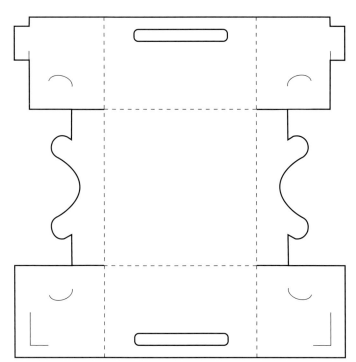

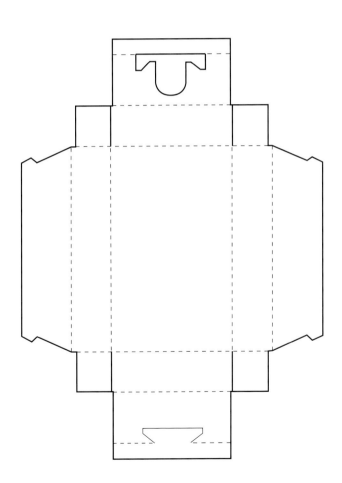

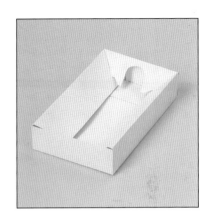

Tray with Bottle Support 107

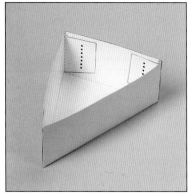

Triangular Tray

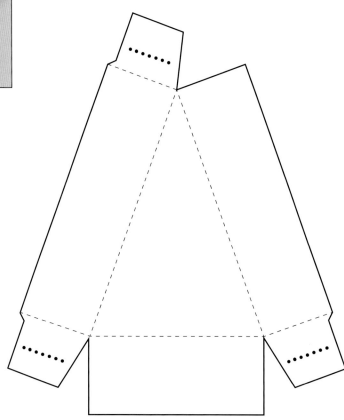

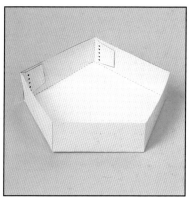

Pentagonal Tray 109

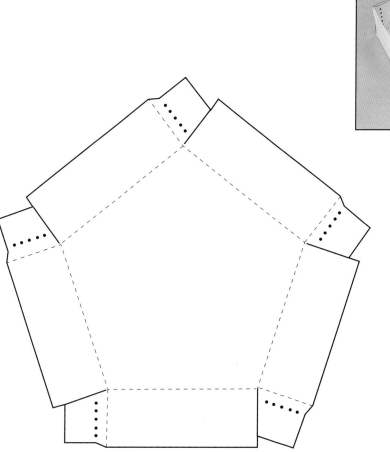

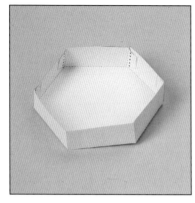

110 **Hexagonal Tray**

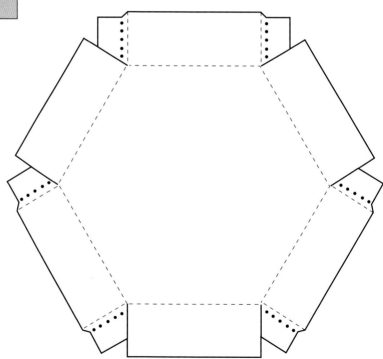

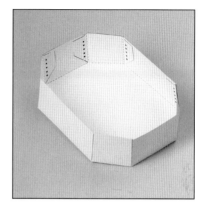

Soft Corner Tray 111

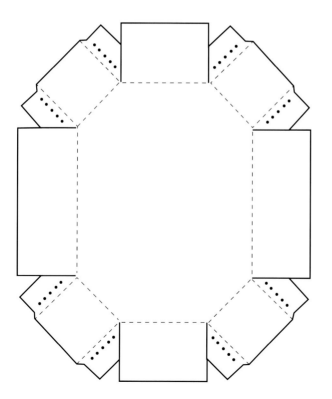

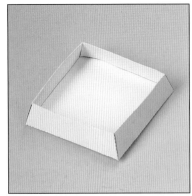

Tapered Tray

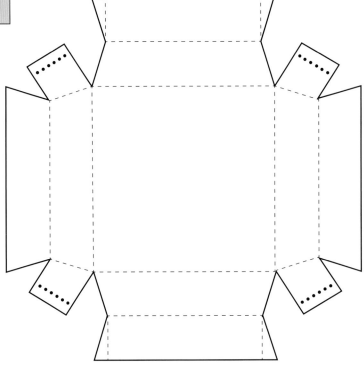

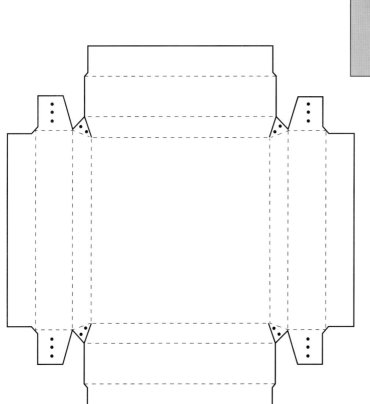

Angled Side Panels 113

114 **Half-Closed Tray with Window**

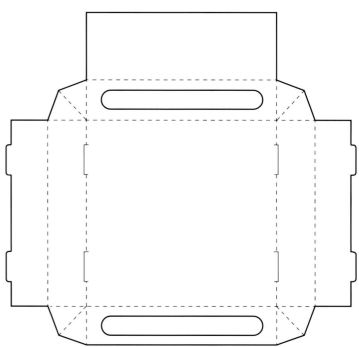

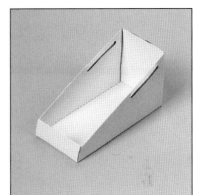

Display Tray 115

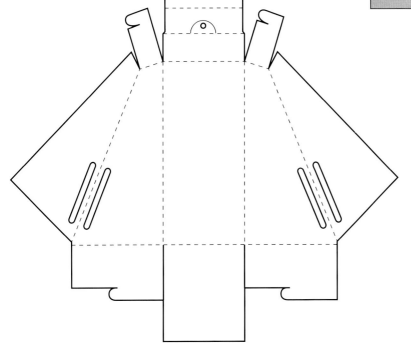

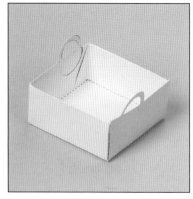

Display Tray

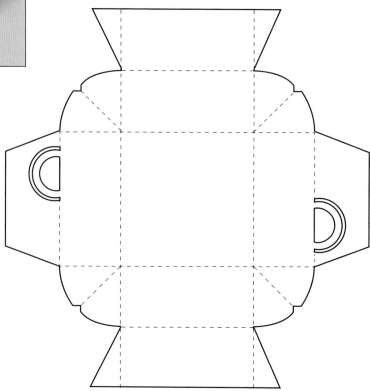

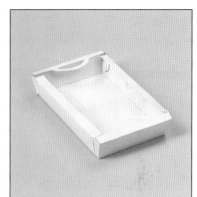

Display Tray   117

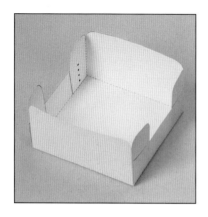

Display Tray

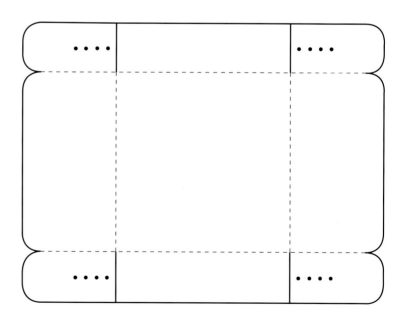

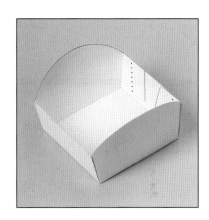

Display Tray   119

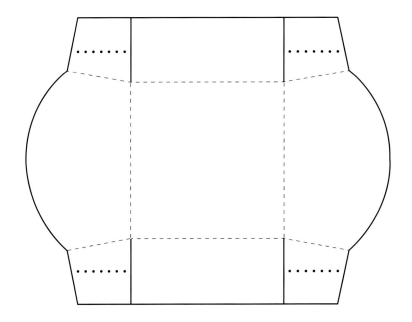

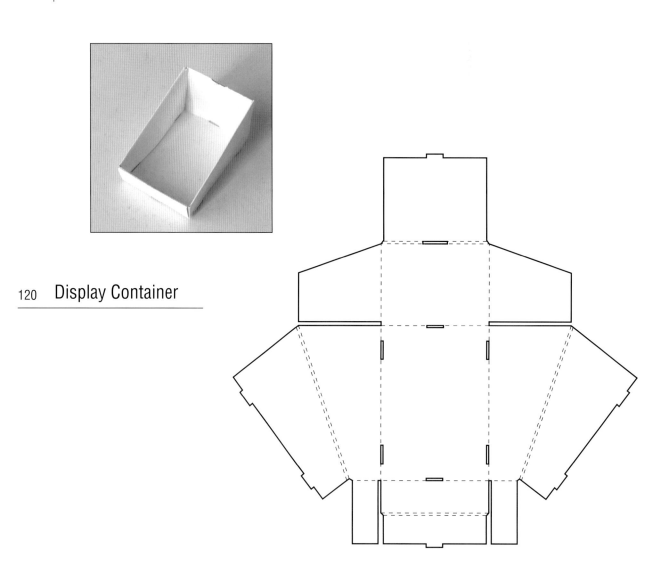

Display Container

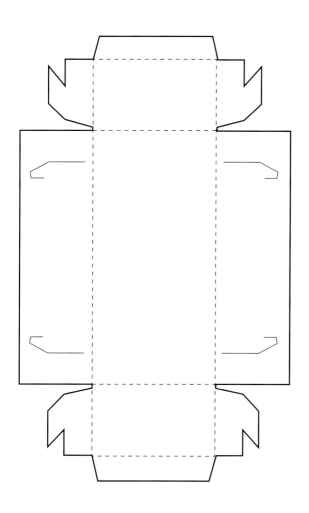

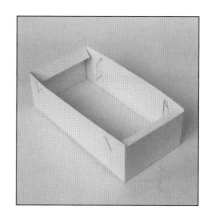

Display Container 121

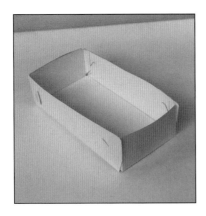

Display Container

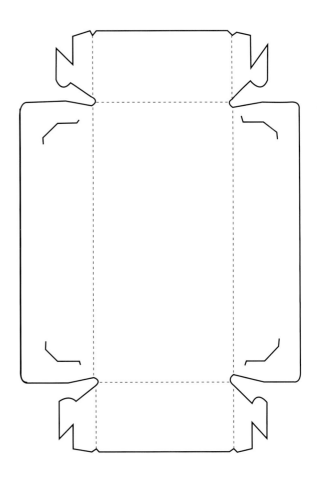

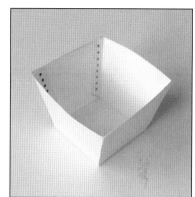

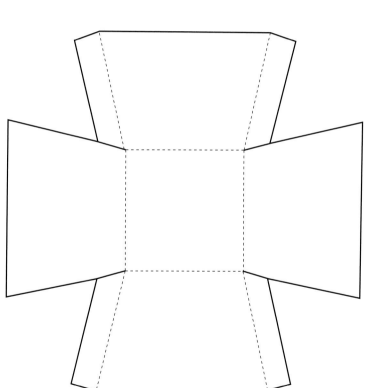

Display Container 123

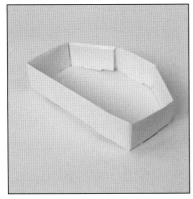

Display Container

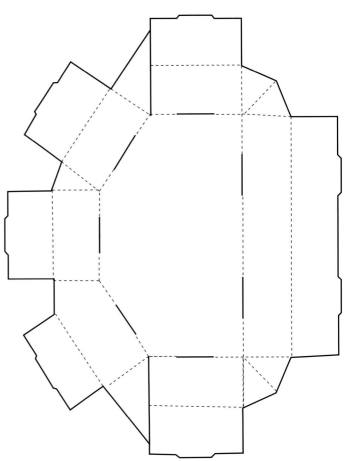

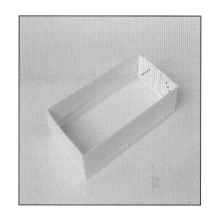

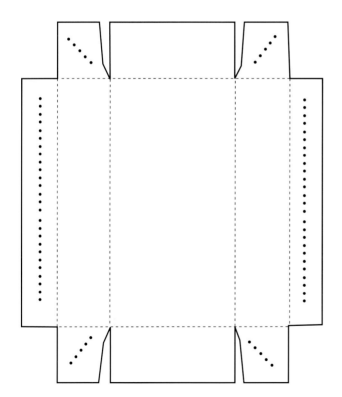

Display Container 125

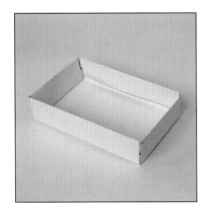

Display Container

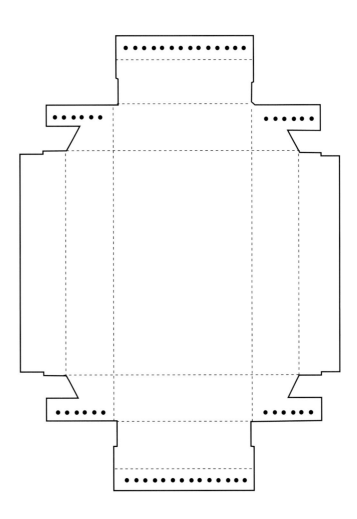

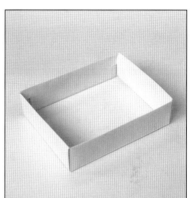

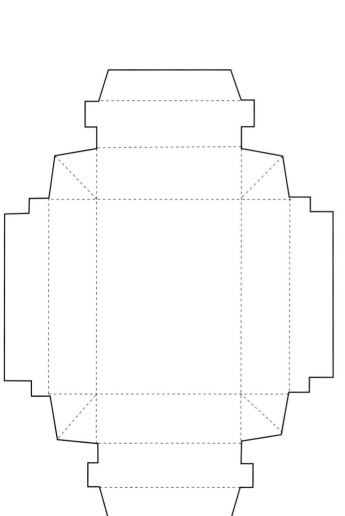

Display Container 127

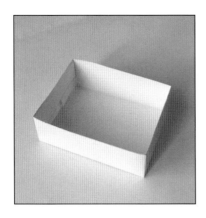

Display Container

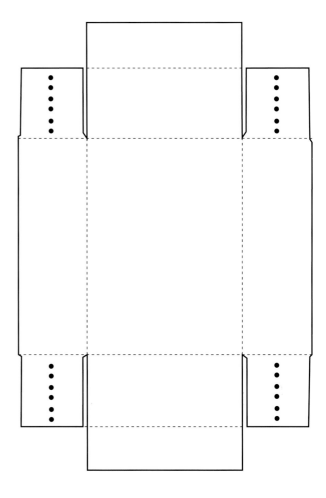

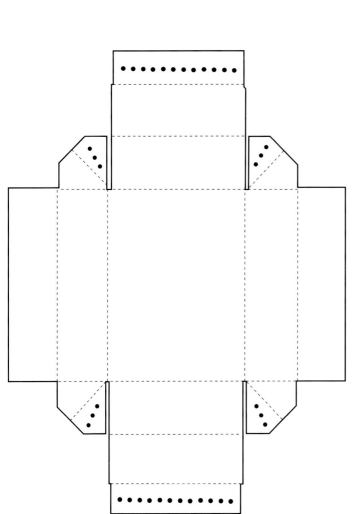

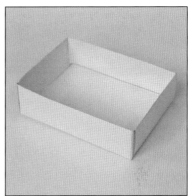

Display Container   129

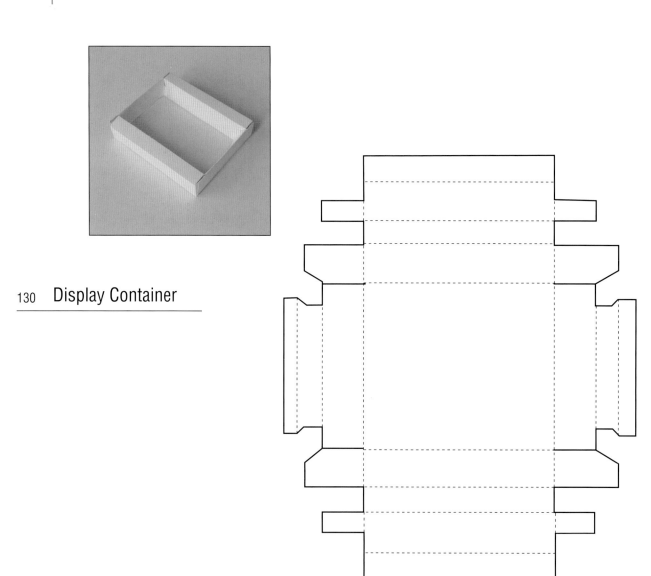

130   Display Container

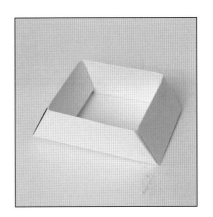

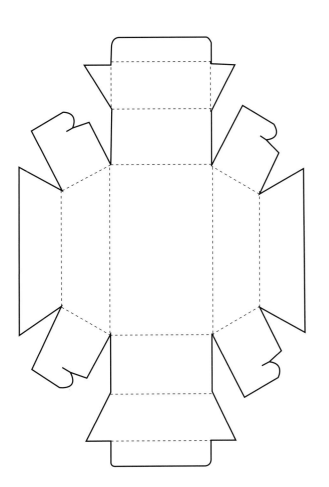

Display Container   131

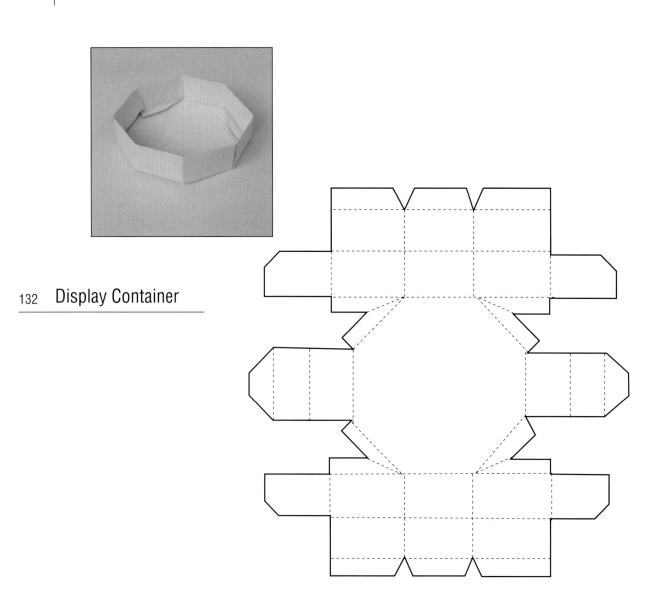

132   Display Container

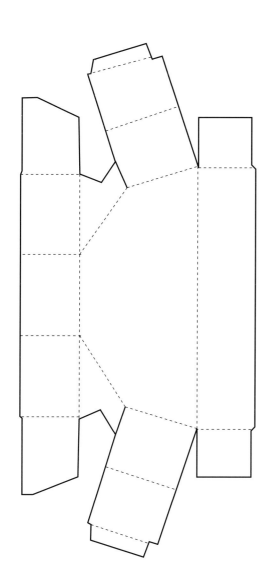

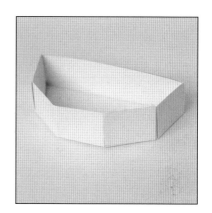

Display Container 133

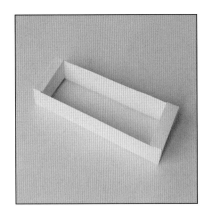

Display Container

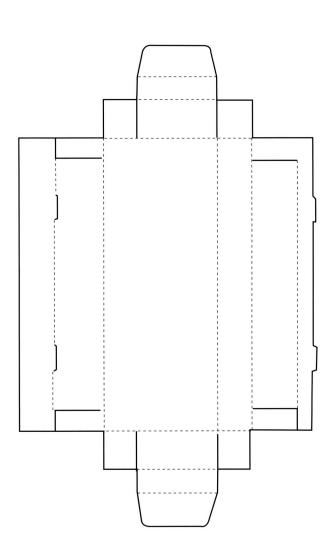

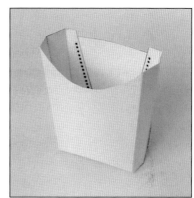

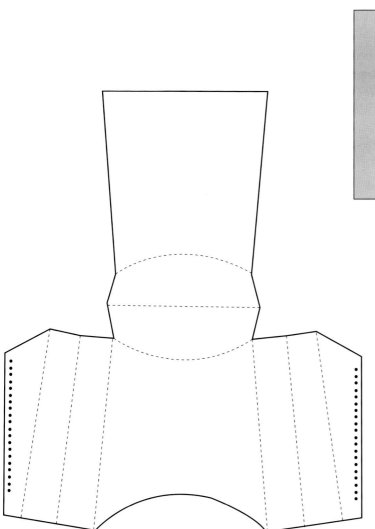

Display Container 135

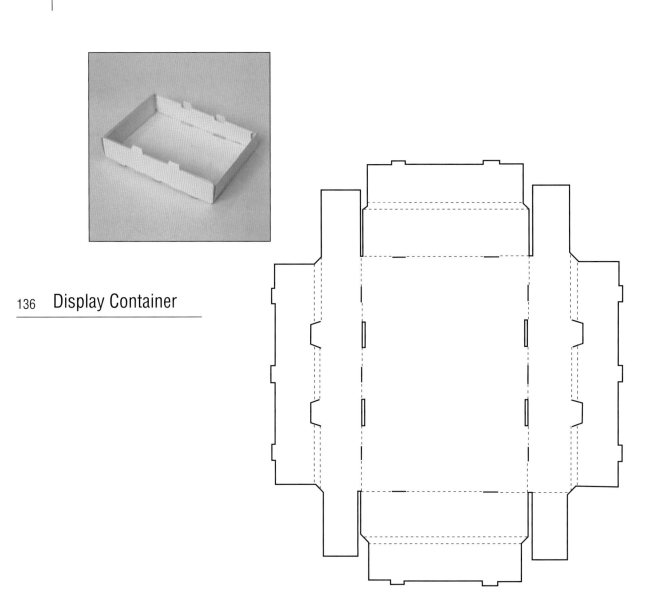

Display Container

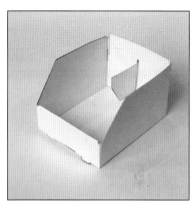

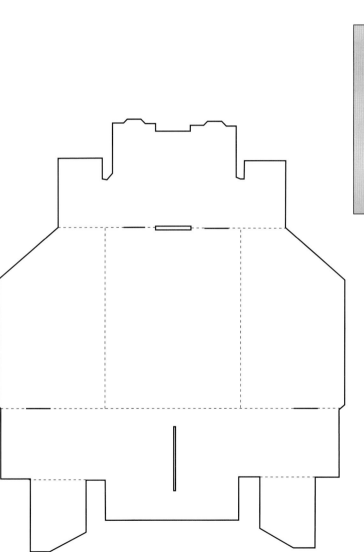

Display Container 137

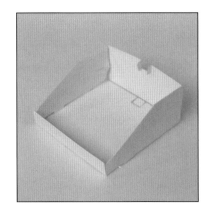

138 Display Container

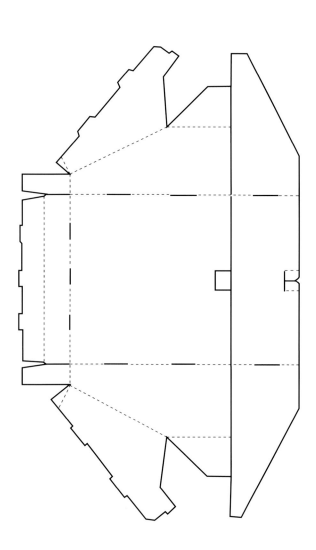

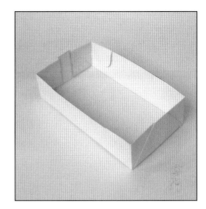

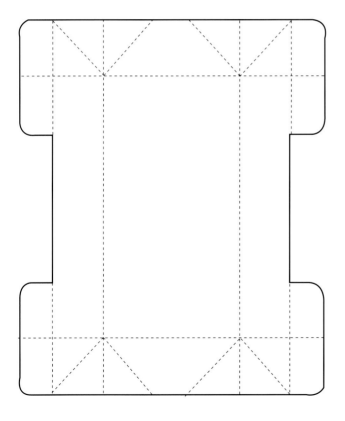

Display Container   139

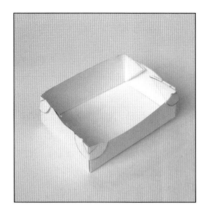

Display Container

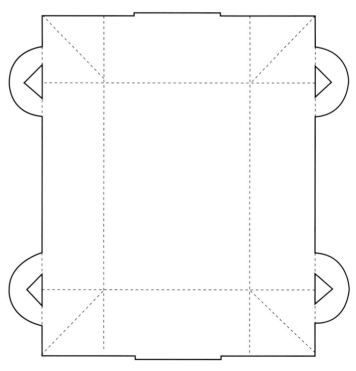

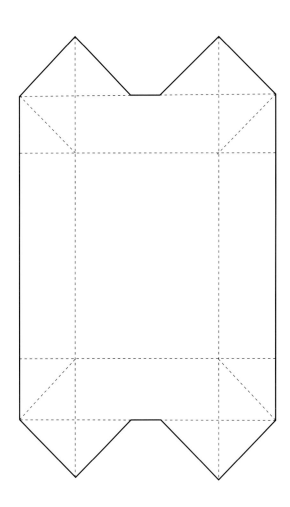

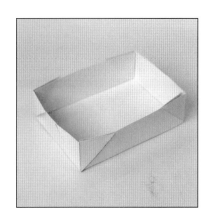

Display Container 141

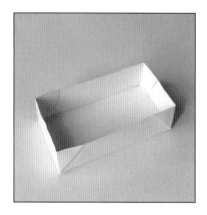

142 Display Container

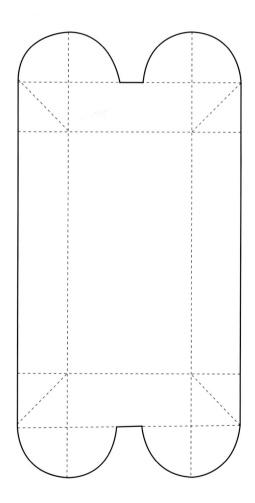

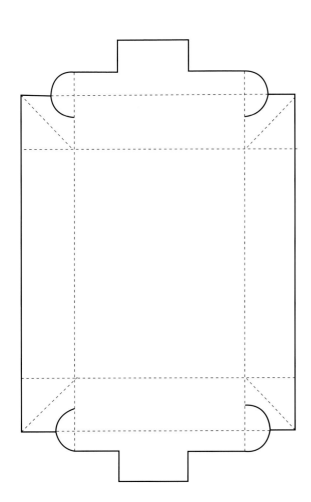

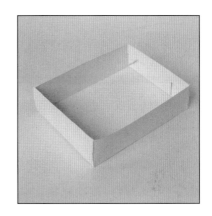

Display Container 143

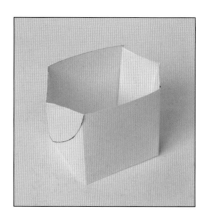

144 Display Container

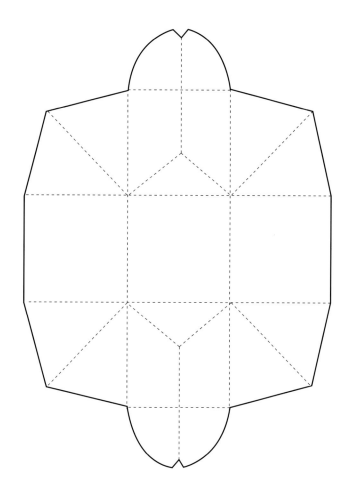

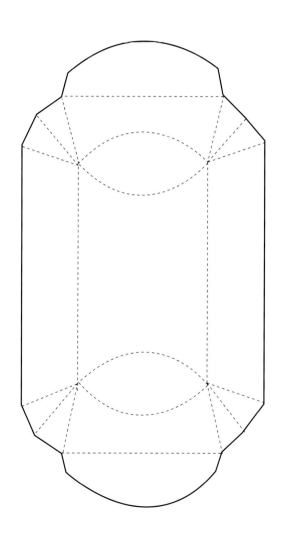

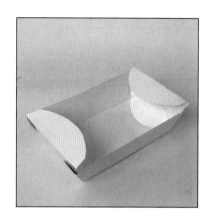

Display Container   145

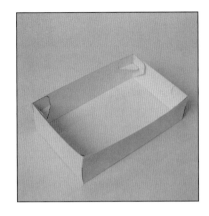

Display Container

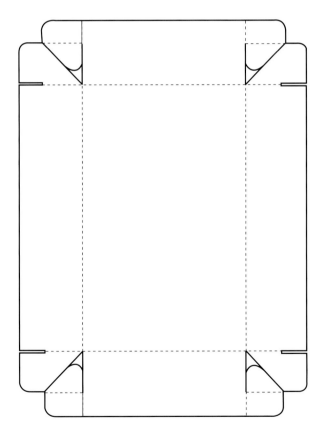

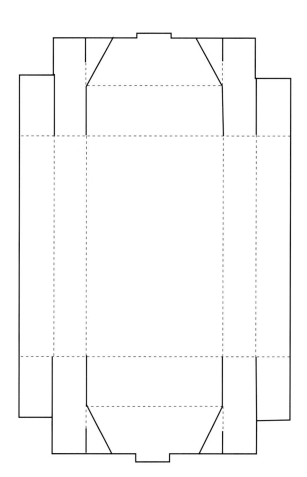

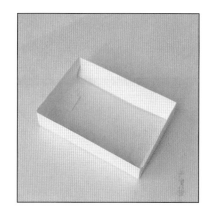

Display Container 147

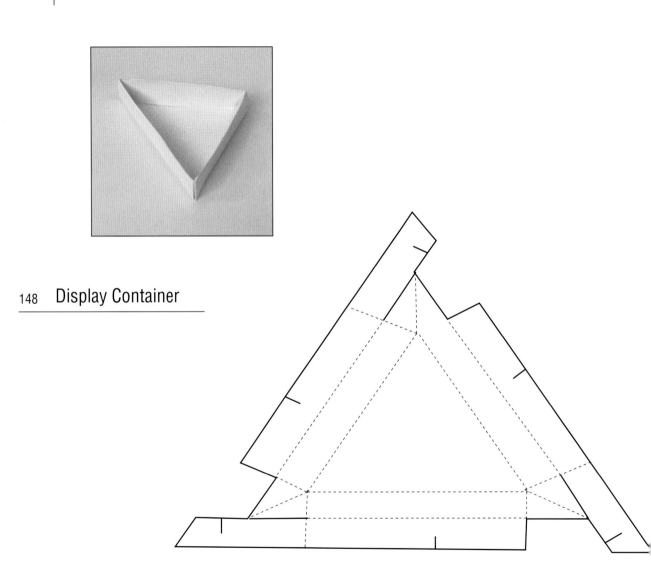

148 Display Container

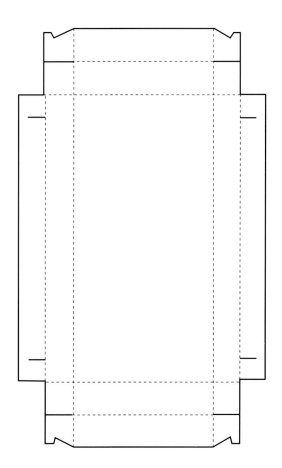

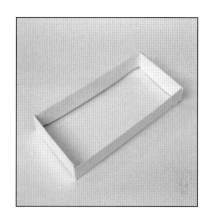

Display Container   149

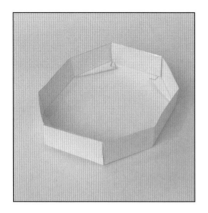

150 Display Container

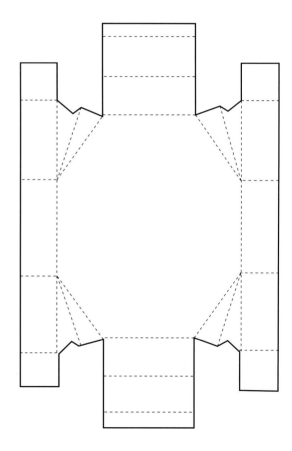

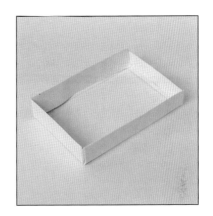

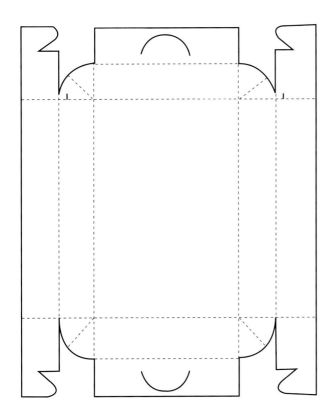

Display Container   151

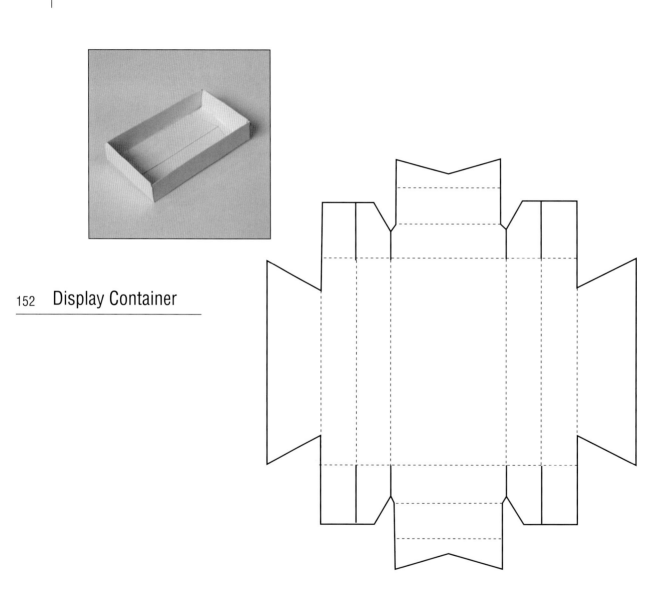

152 Display Container

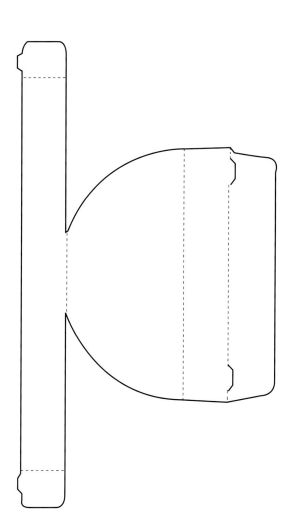

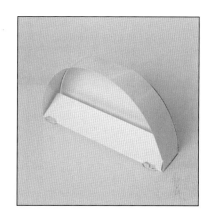

Display Container 153

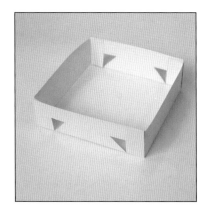

154   Display Container

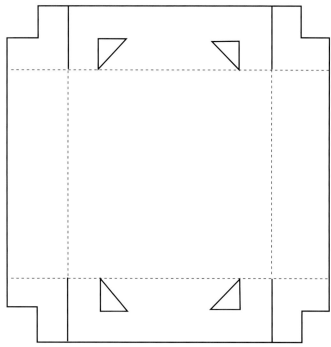

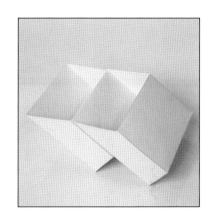

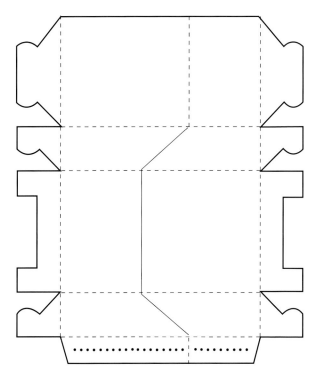

Display Container   155

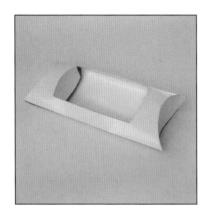

156 Display Container

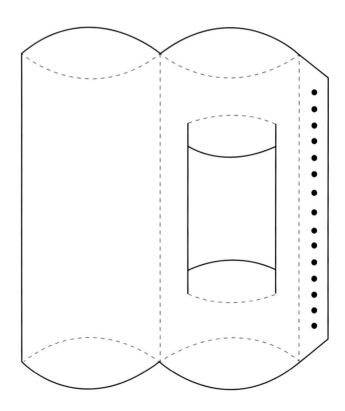

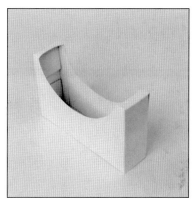

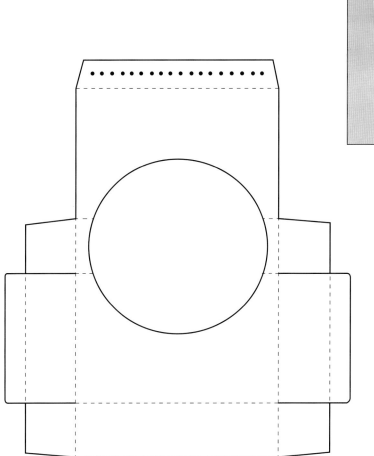

Display Container 157

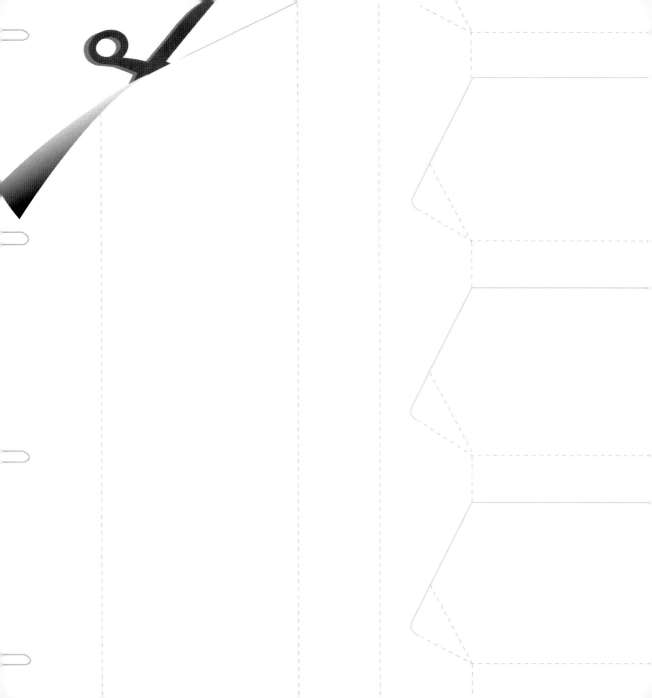

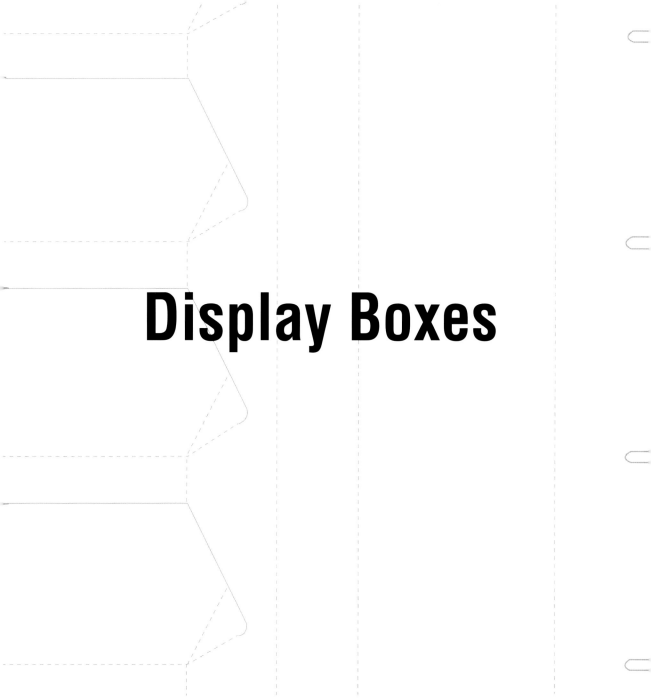

Display Boxes

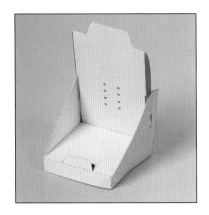

Display Box

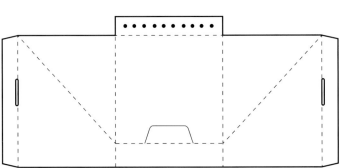

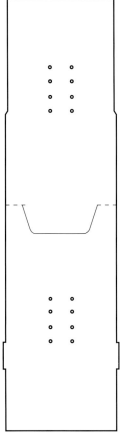

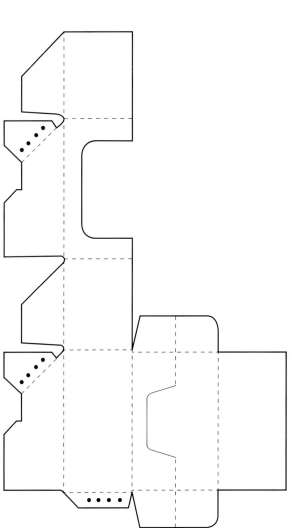

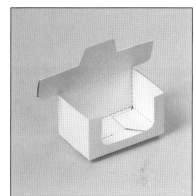

Display Box   161

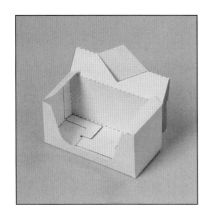

Display Box

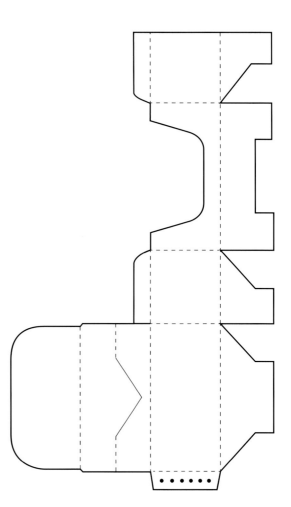

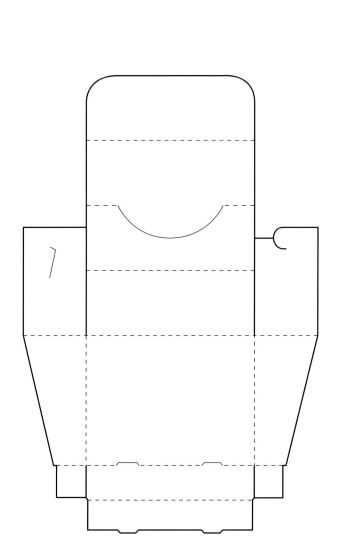

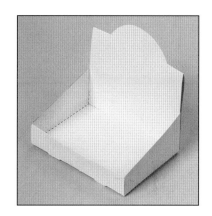

Display Box 163

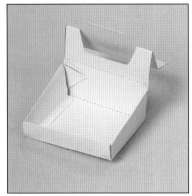

Display Box

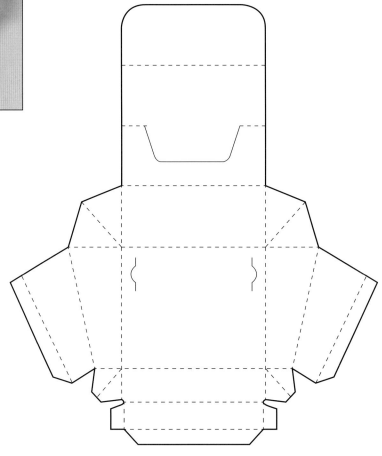

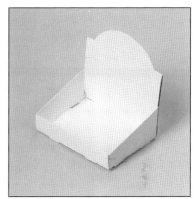

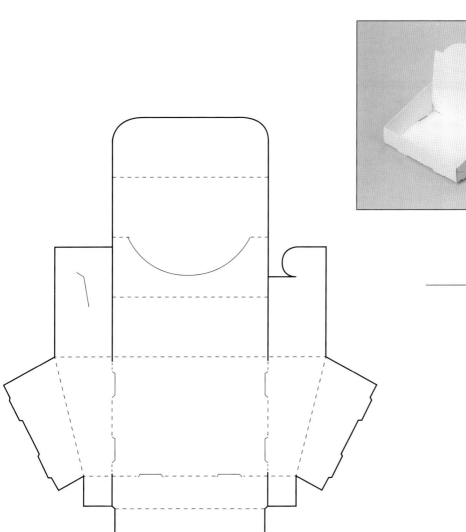

Display Box 165

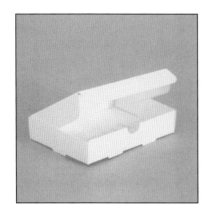

Double-walled Box with Foot Lock

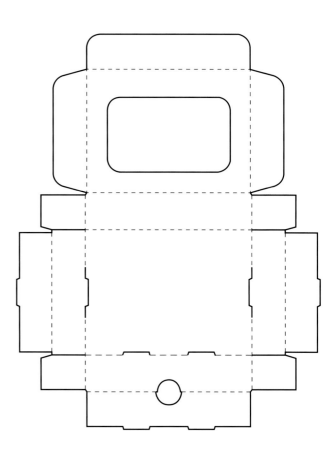

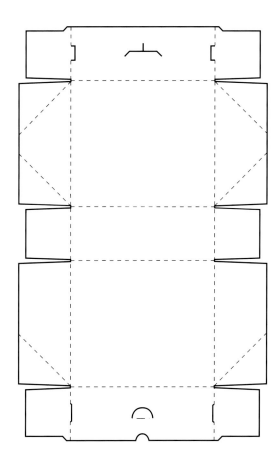

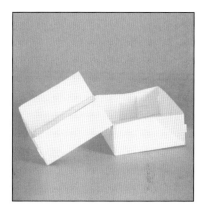

Six-point-glued Box 167

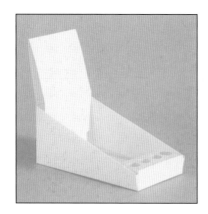

168 Display Box

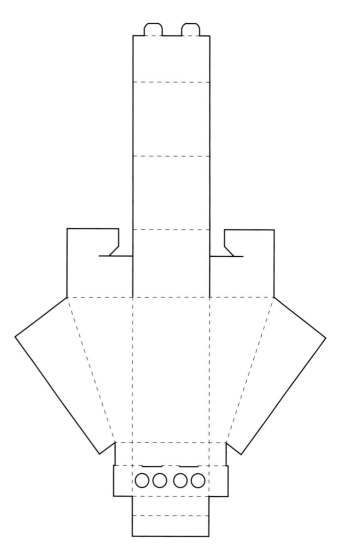

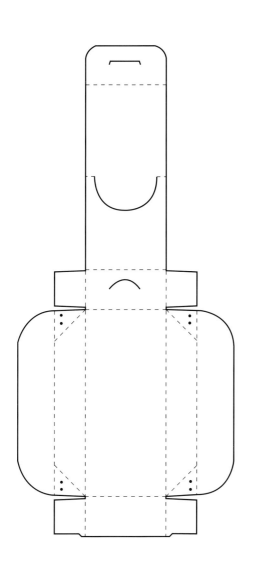

Four-points-glued Display Box   169

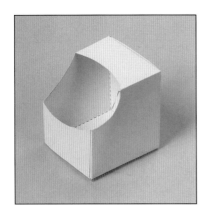

170   Display Box with Window

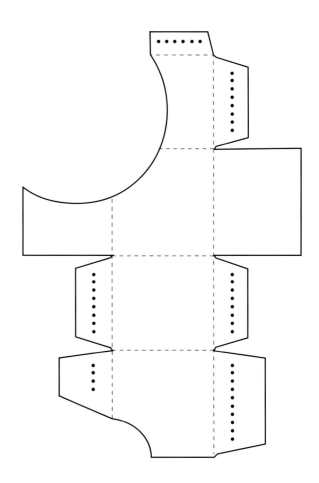

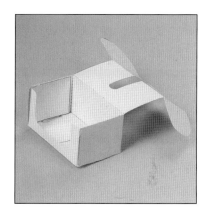

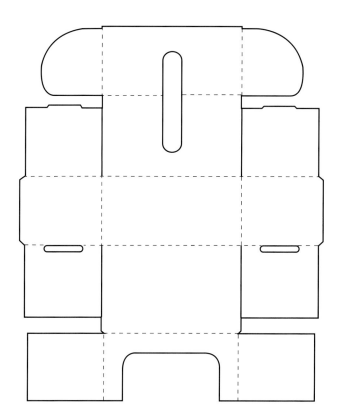

Box with Display Slit   171

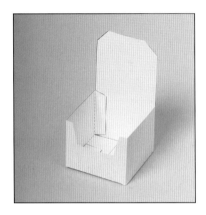

Display Box

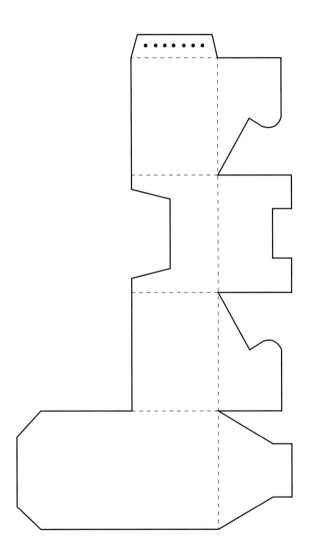

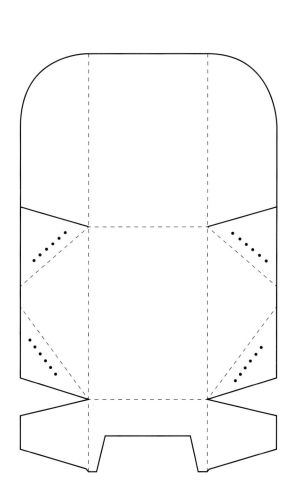

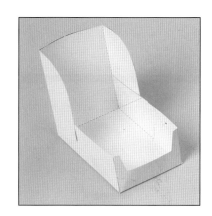

Display Box   173

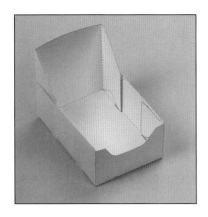

174 Display Box

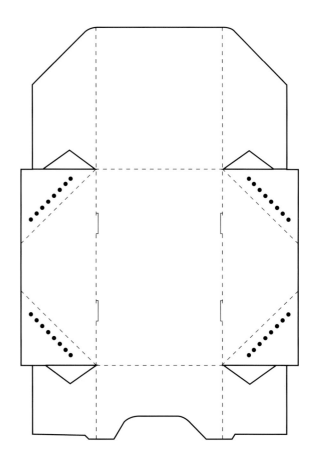

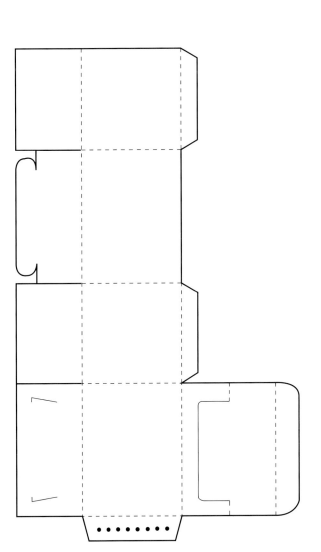

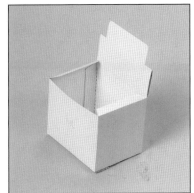

Display Box   175

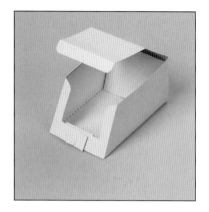

Display Box

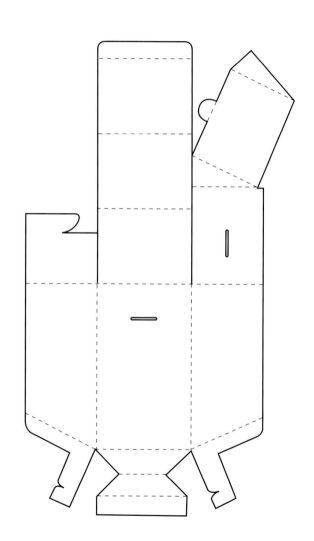

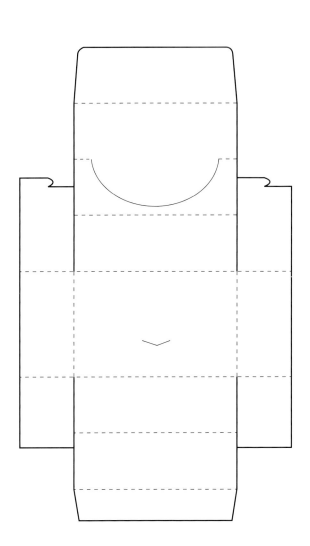

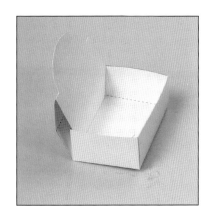

Display Box   177

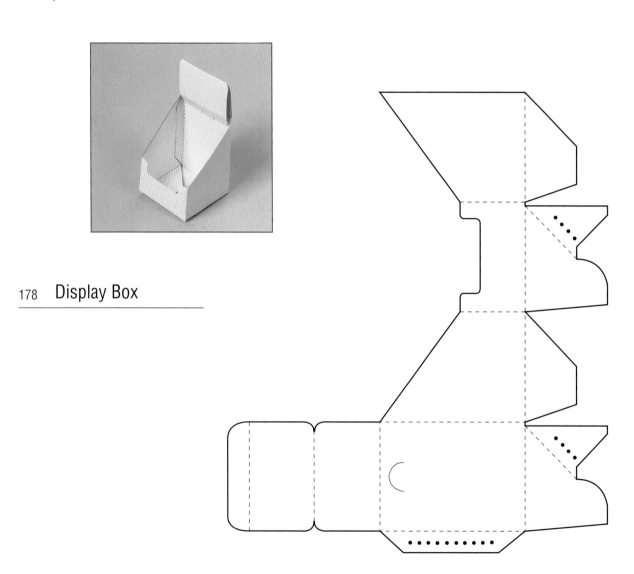

Display Box

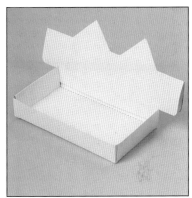

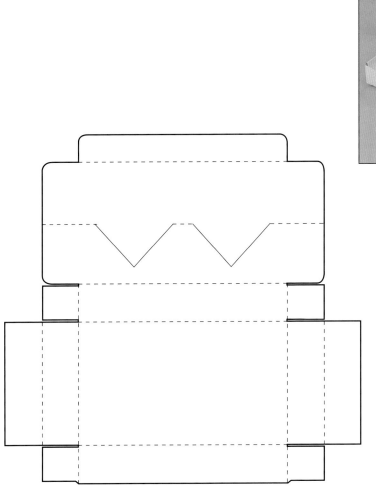

Display Box   179

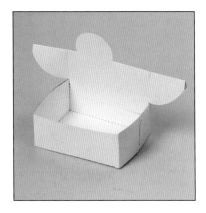

Display Box

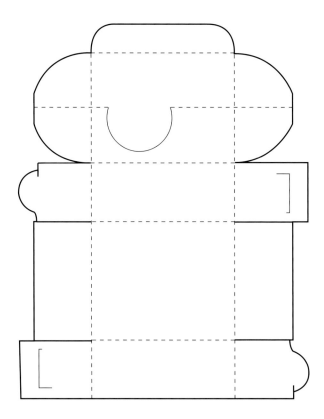

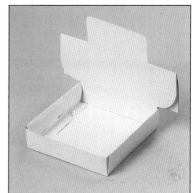

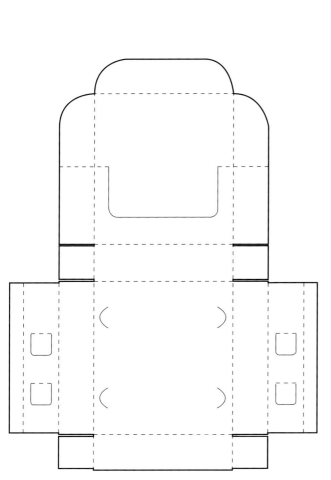

Display Box   181

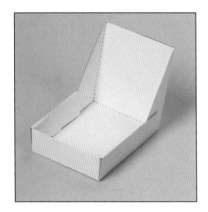

Display Box

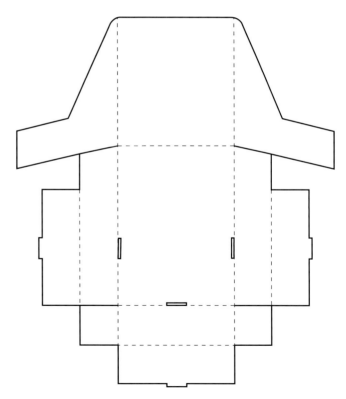

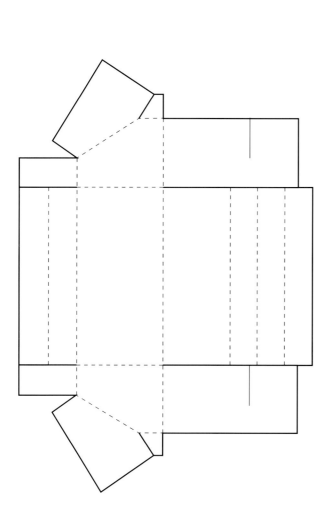

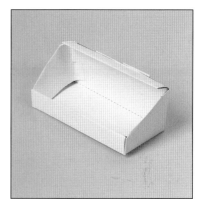

Display Box   183

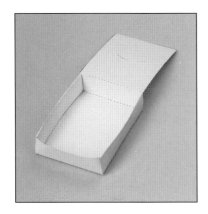

184   Display Box

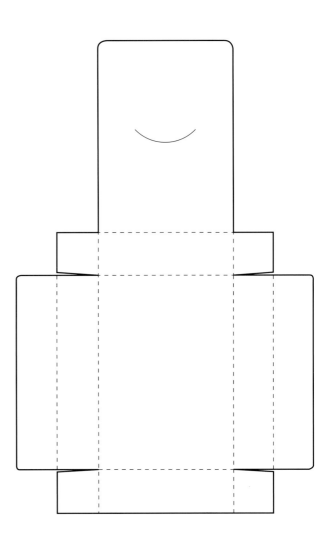

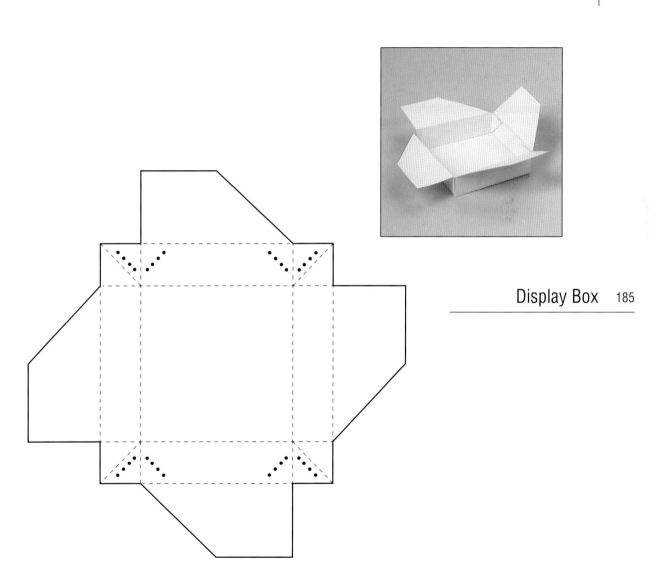

Display Box   185

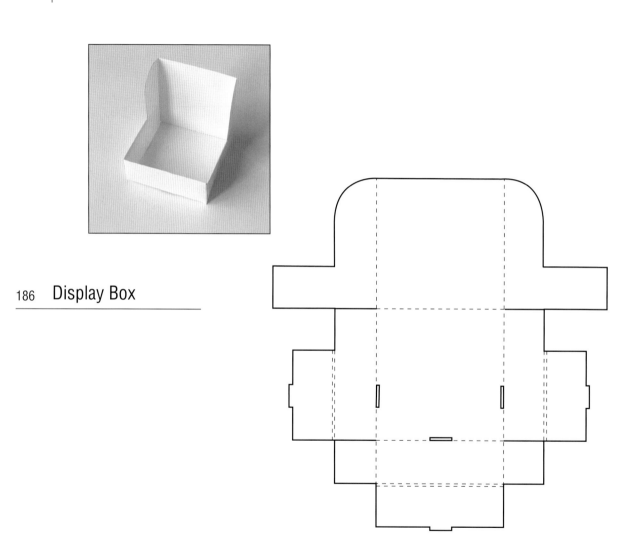

Display Box

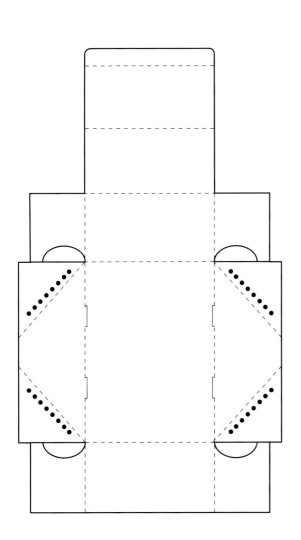

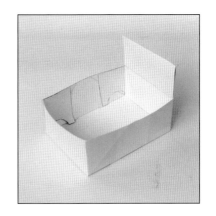

Display Box   187

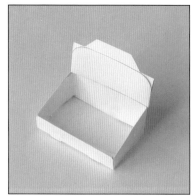

188 Display Box with Foot Lock

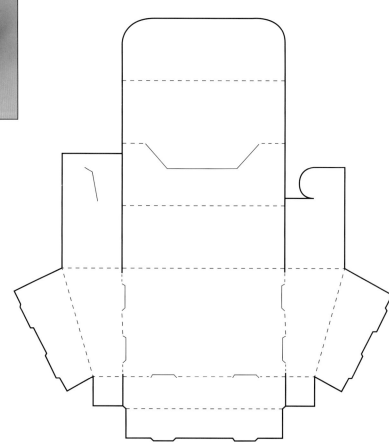

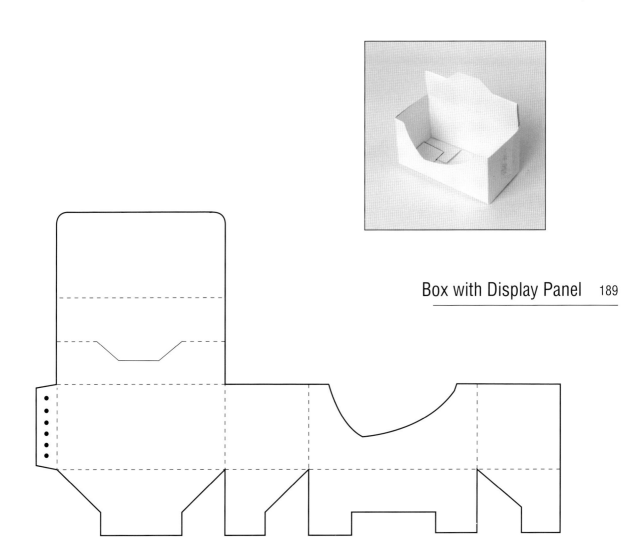

Box with Display Panel 189

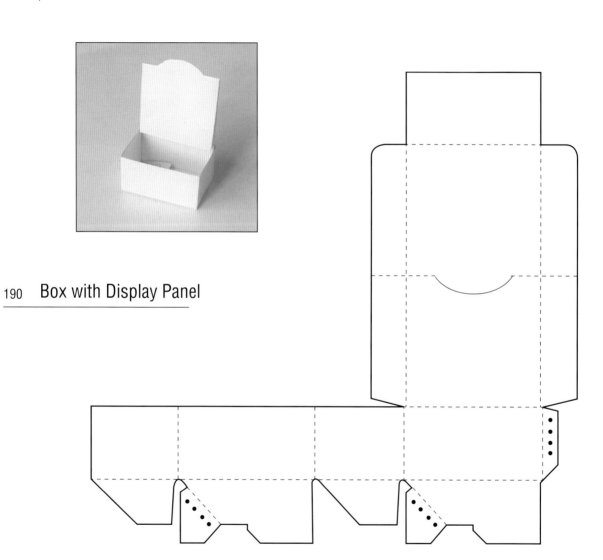

Box with Display Panel

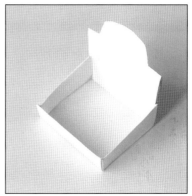

Box with Display Panel 191

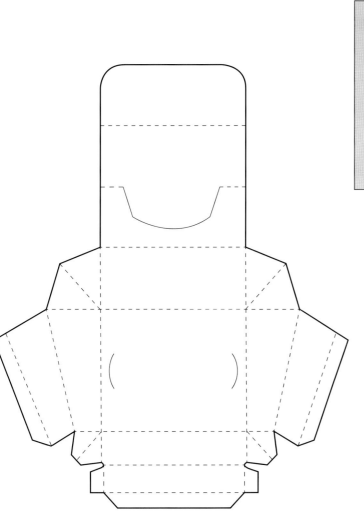

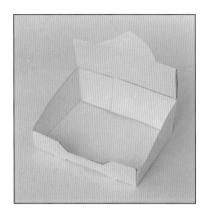

Box with Display Panel

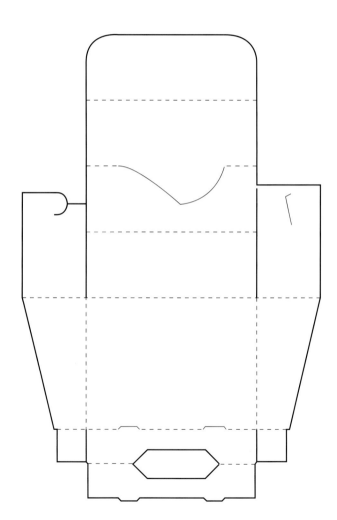

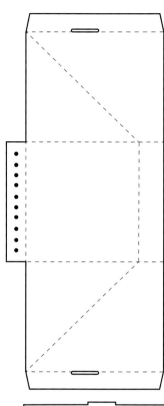

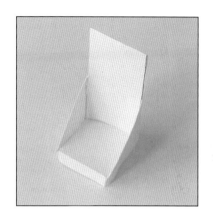

Display Box 193

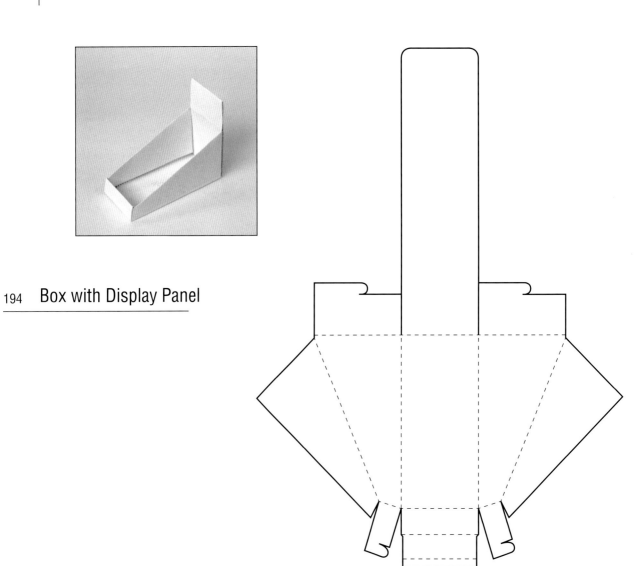

Box with Display Panel

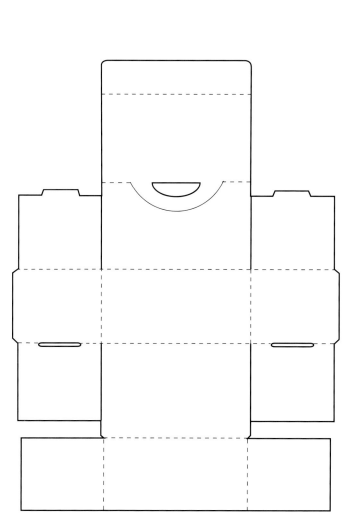

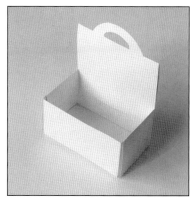

Back Panel with Hanging Hole   195

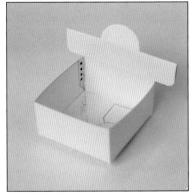

Box with Display Panel

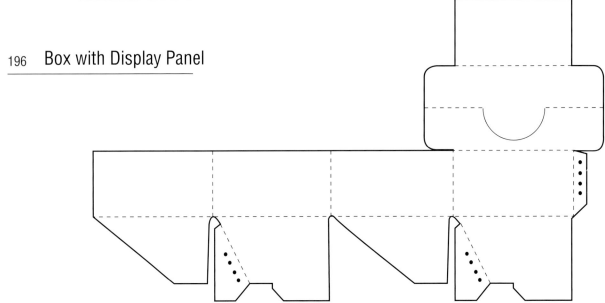

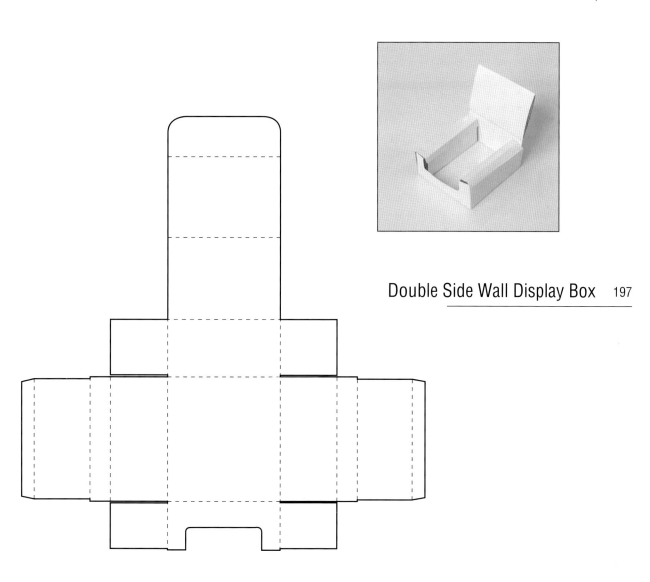

Double Side Wall Display Box 197

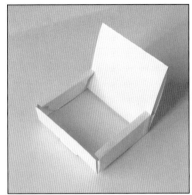

Double Side Wall Display Box

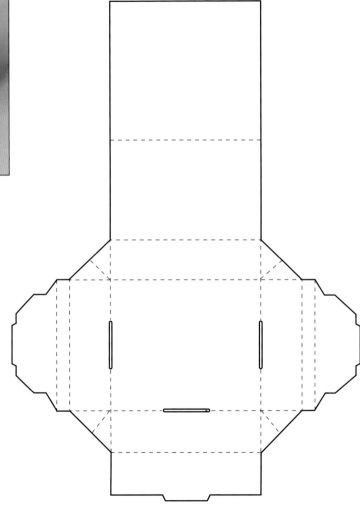

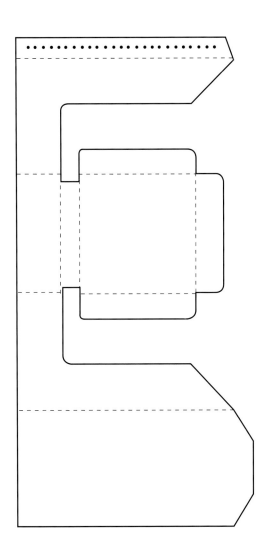

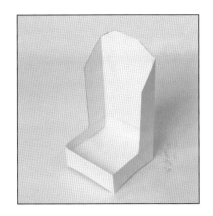

Candle Display Box   199

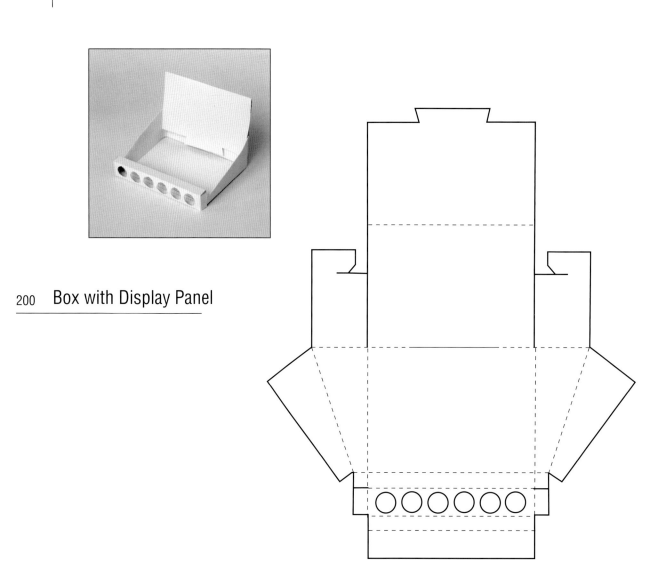

200 **Box with Display Panel**

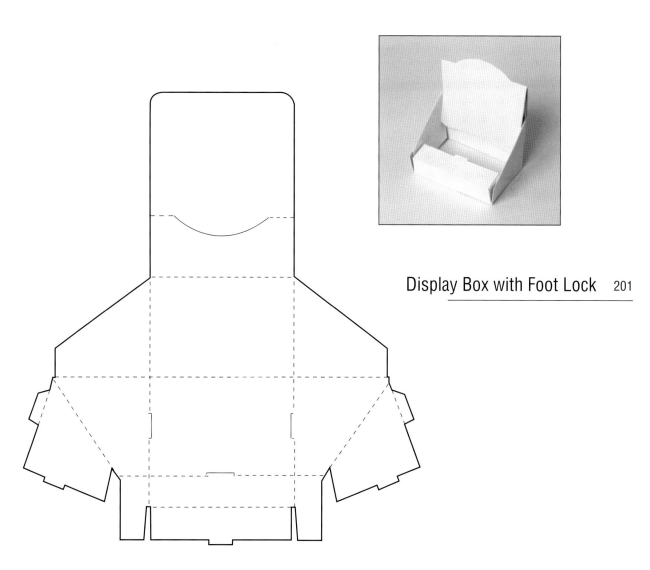

Display Box with Foot Lock   201

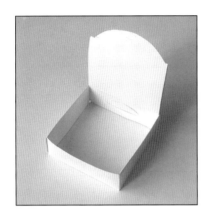

202 Four-points-glued Display Box

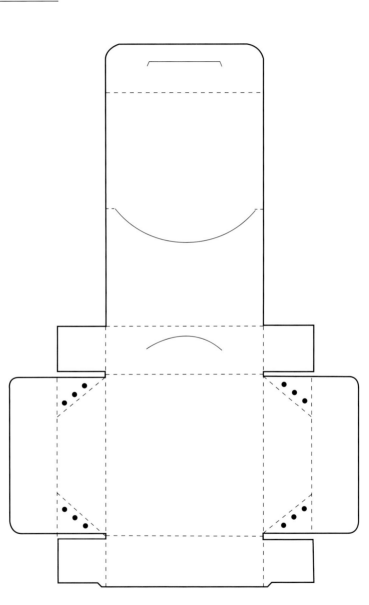

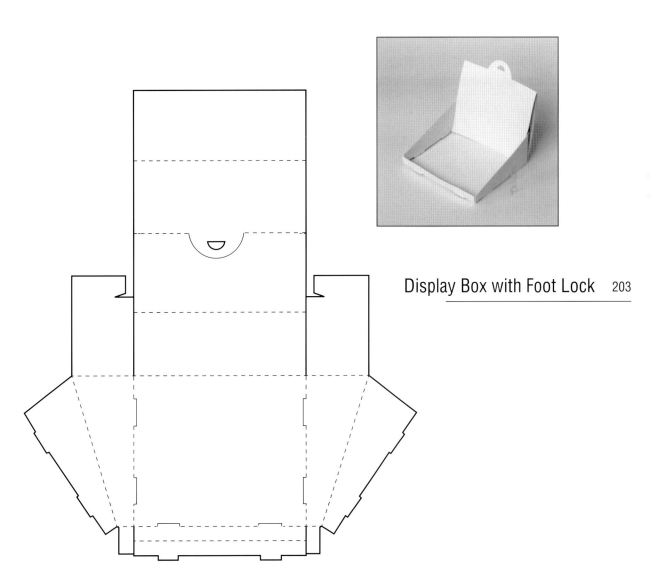

Display Box with Foot Lock 203

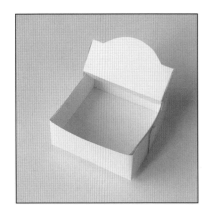

Display Box

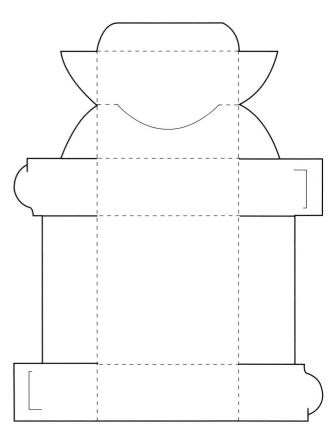

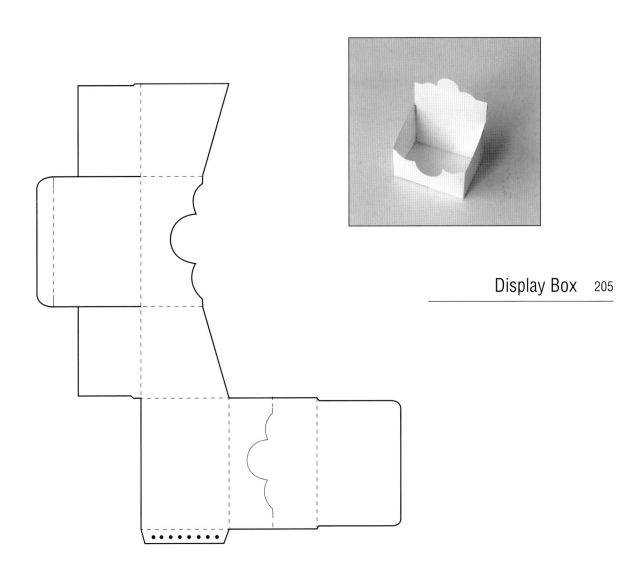

Display Box 205

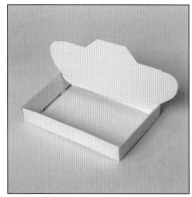

206 Display Box

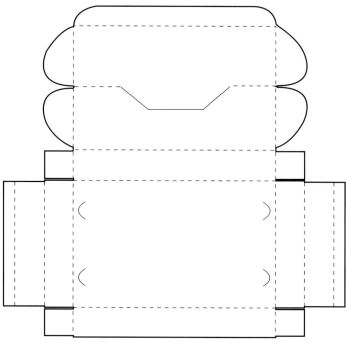

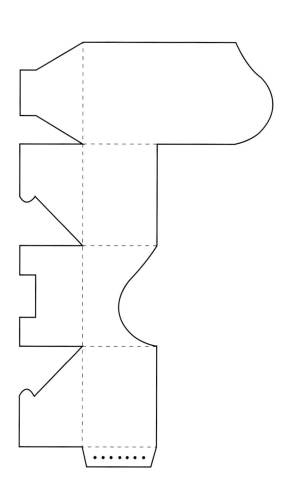

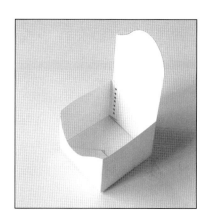

Display Box   207

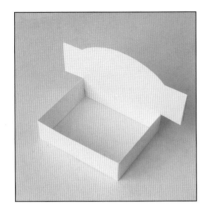

208 Box with Display Panel

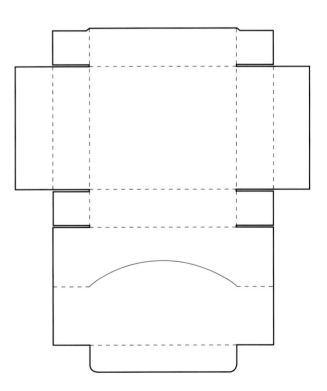

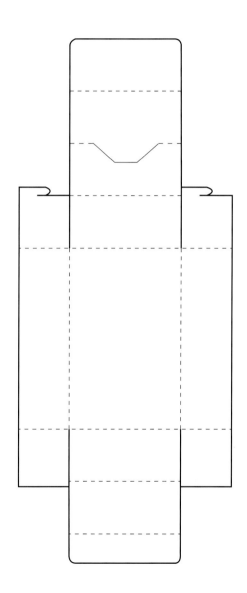

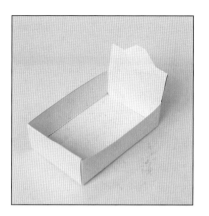

Box with Display Panel 209

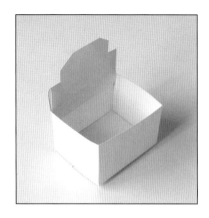

210 Box with Display Panel

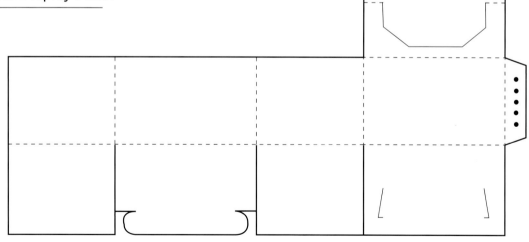

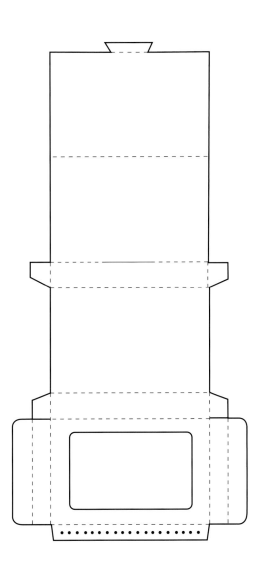

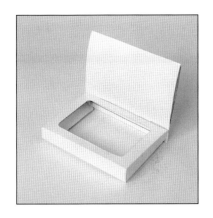

Book-shaped Window Box 211

212 Frame-shaped Book Box

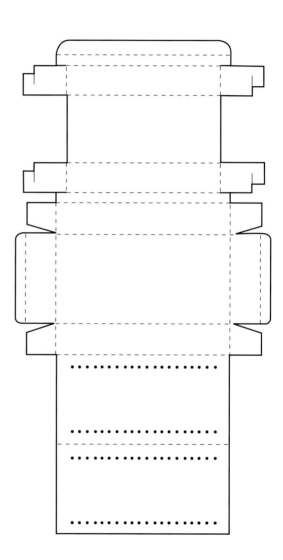

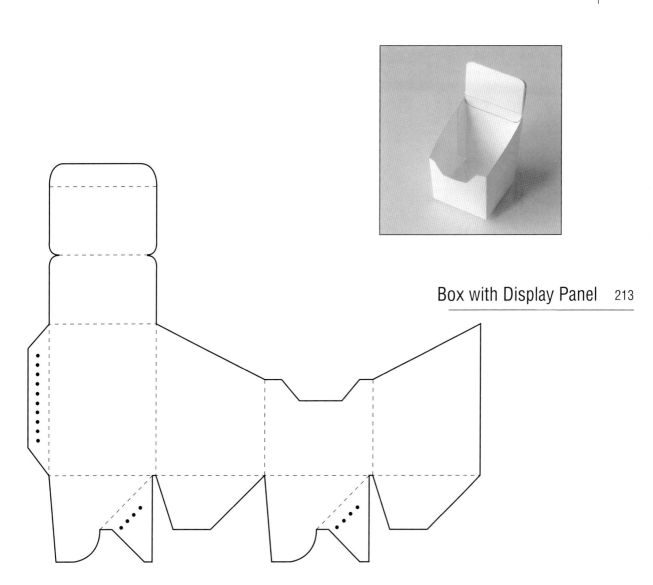

Box with Display Panel 213

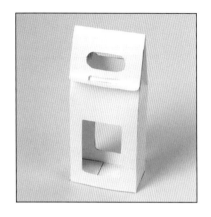

214 Special Style Display Box

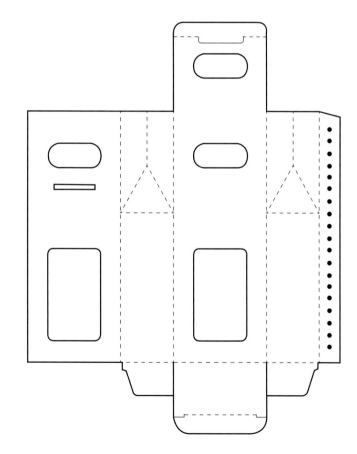

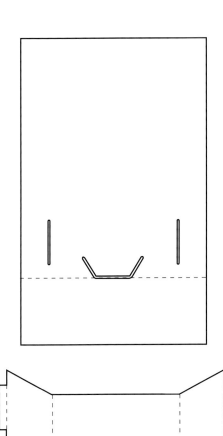

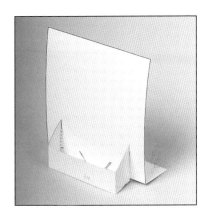

Pocket Easel with Rifle Lock   215

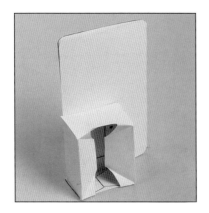

Dispenser with Extended Back Panel

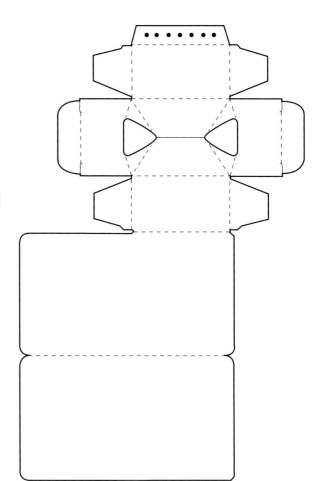

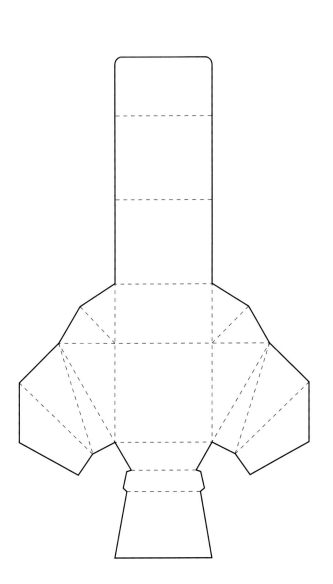

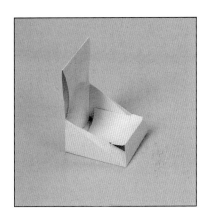

Display Container   217

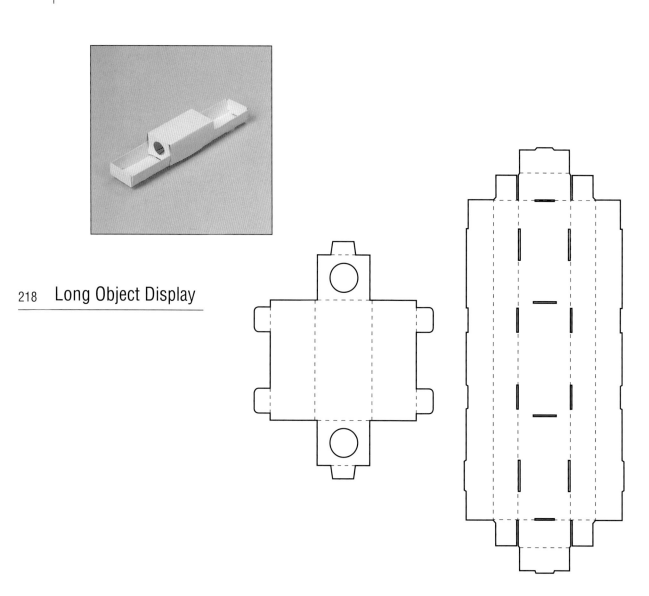

Long Object Display

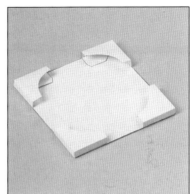

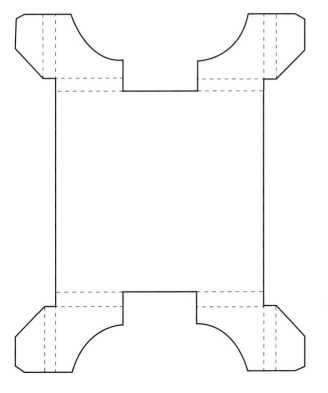

Frame Support 219

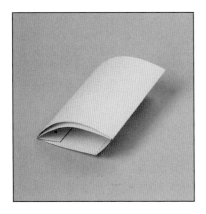

220 **Special Style Display Box**

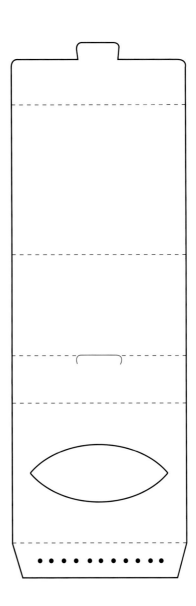

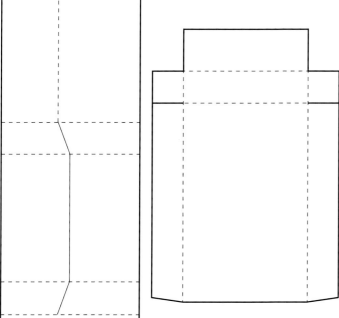

Display Box with Flip Top 221

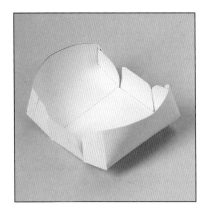

Special Style Display Box

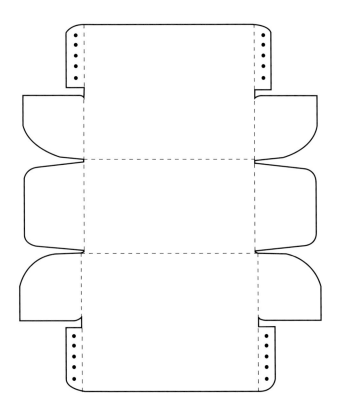

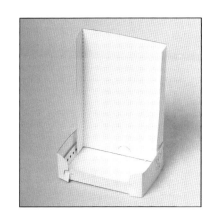

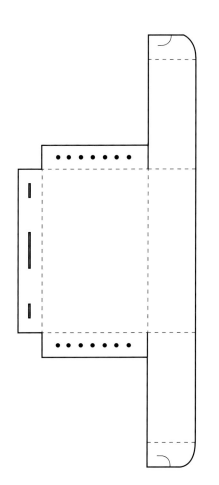

Display Container 223

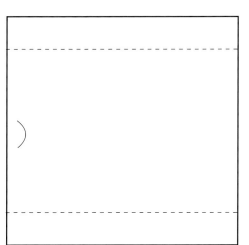

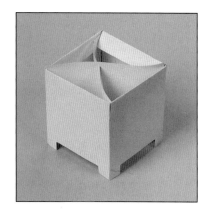

Dividing Display Box

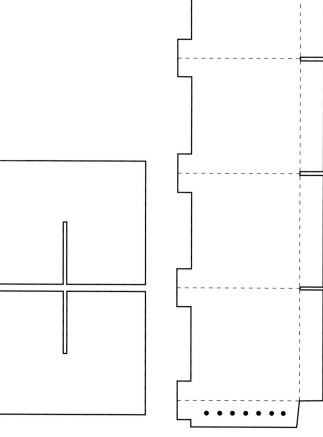

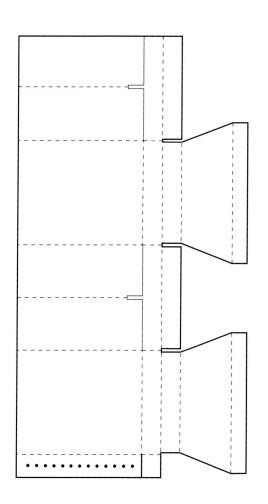

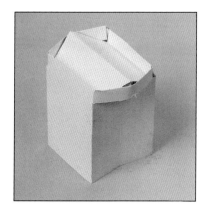

Special Style Display Box 225

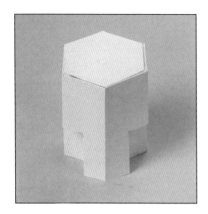

226 Special Style Display Box

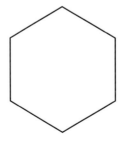

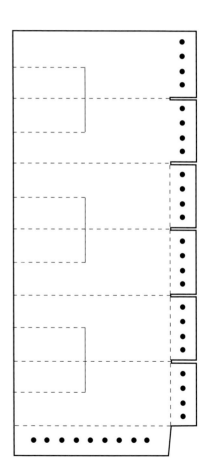

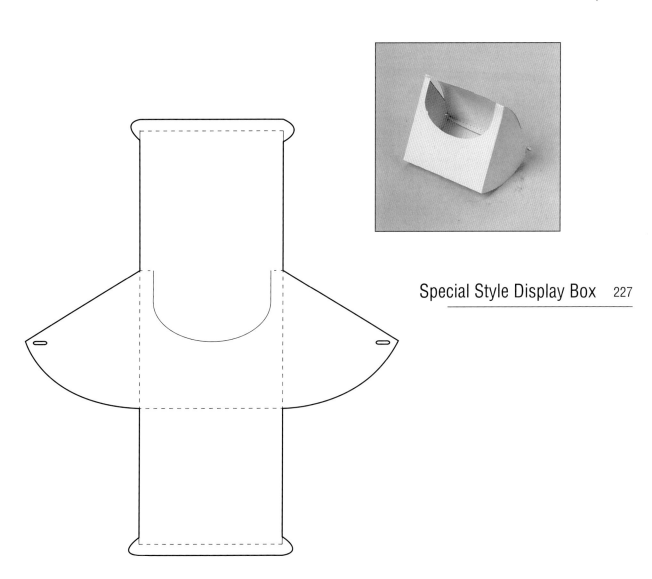

Special Style Display Box   227

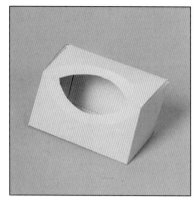

228 Special Style Display Box

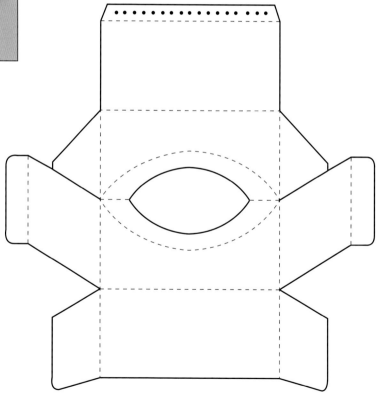

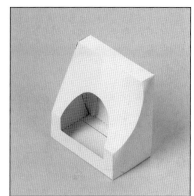

Special Style Display Box 229

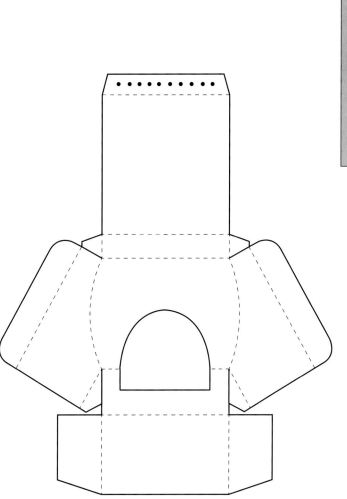

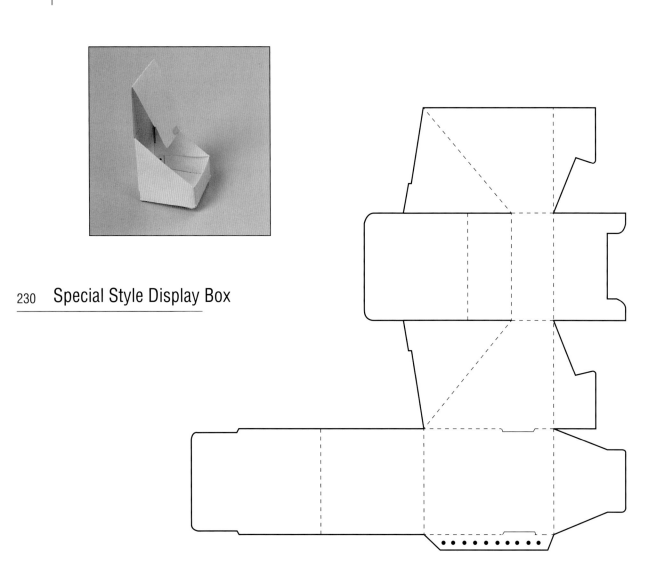

230 Special Style Display Box

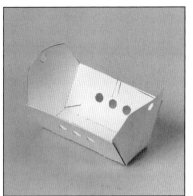

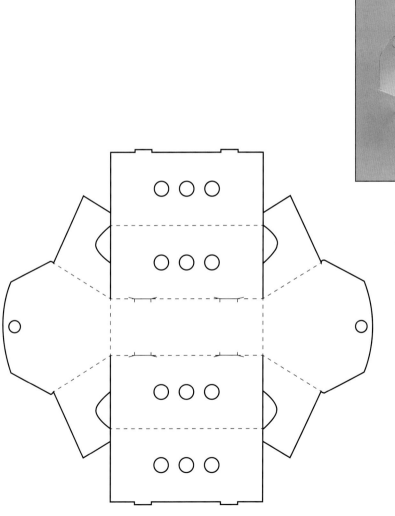

Special Style Display Box 231

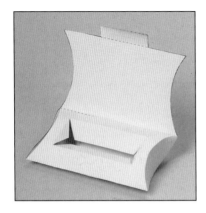

232 Special Style Display Box

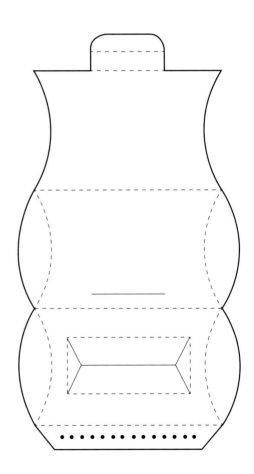

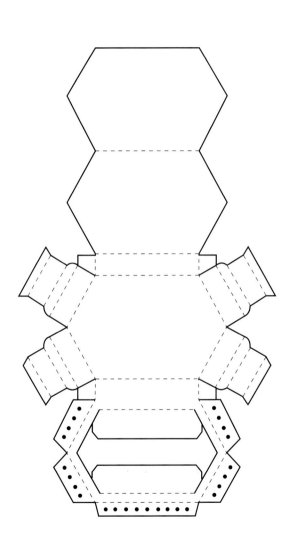

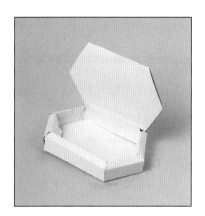

Special Style Display Box   233

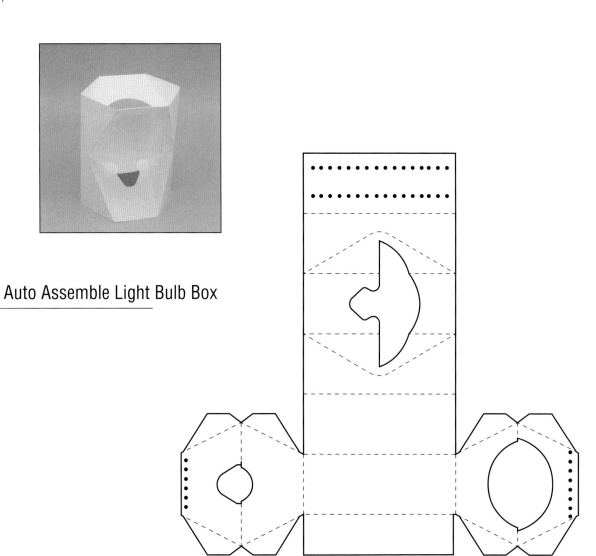

234 Auto Assemble Light Bulb Box

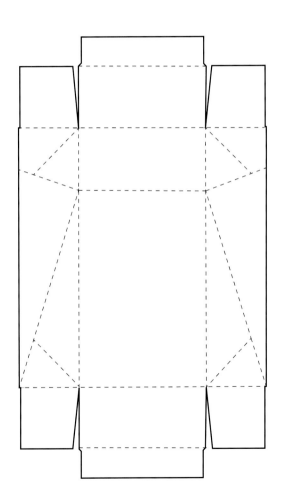

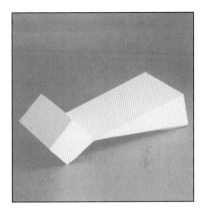

Four-points-glued Display Box   235

Window Boxes

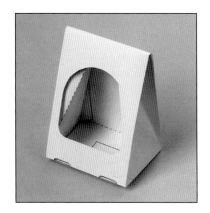

Window Display with Triangular Sides

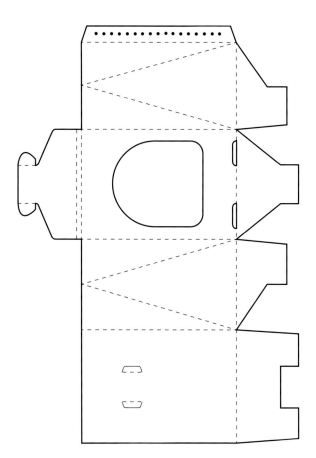

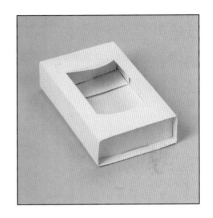

Receding Top and Bottom 239

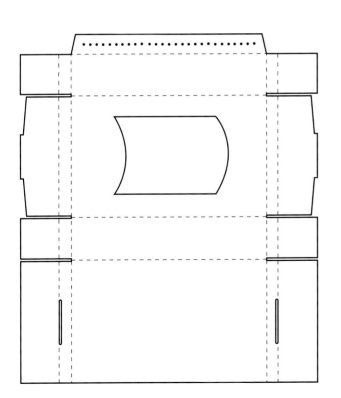

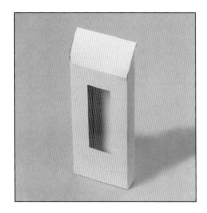

240 Window Box with Receding Top

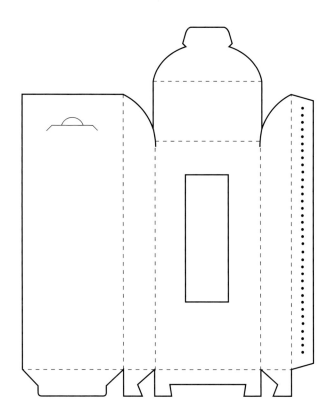

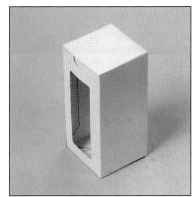

Window Display Box 241

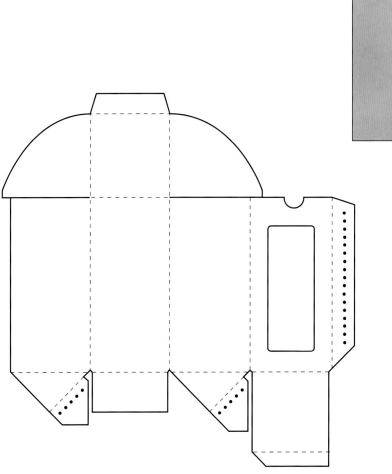

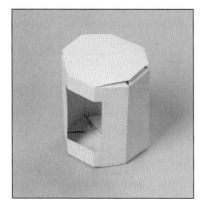

242 Octagonal Box with Window

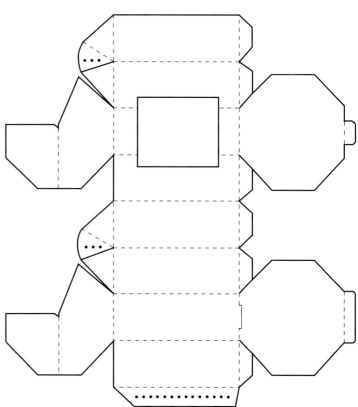

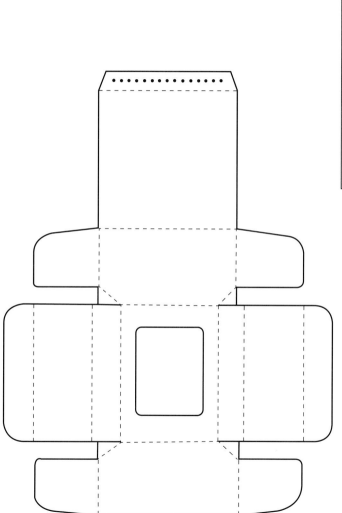

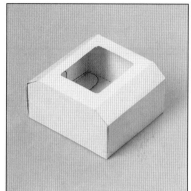

Window Display Box 243

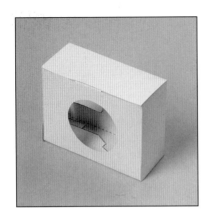

Window Display Box

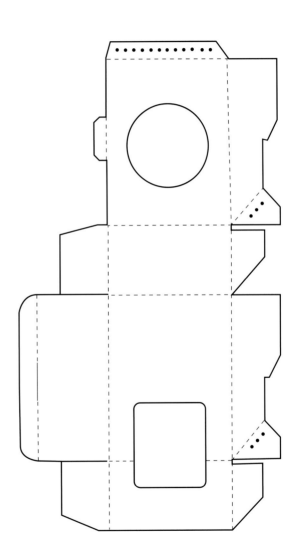

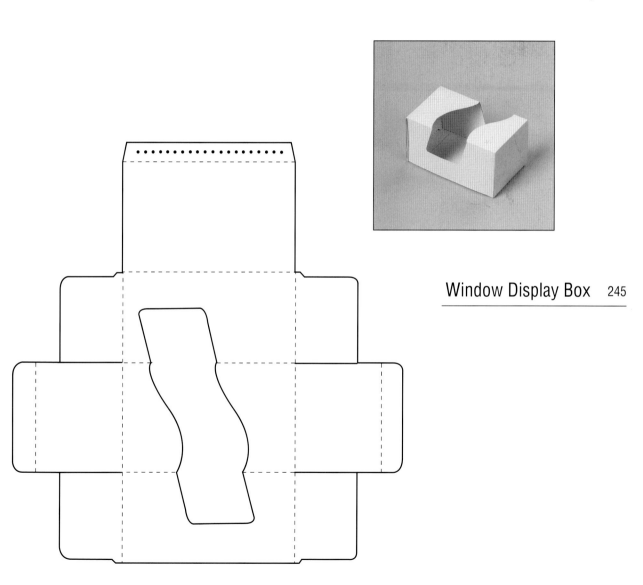

Window Display Box 245

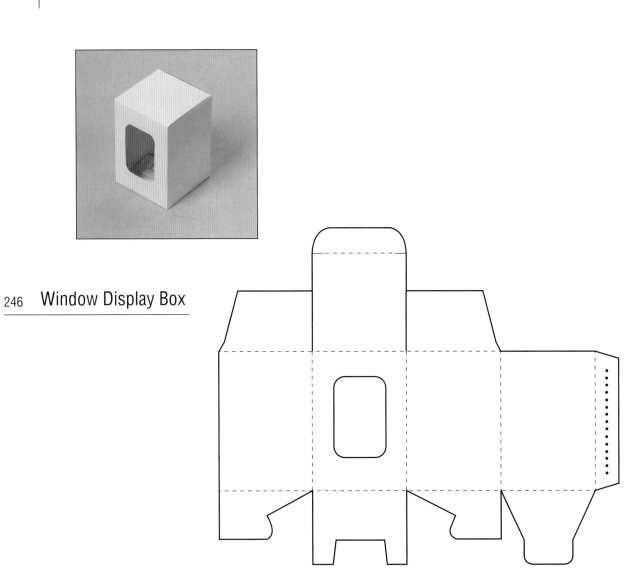

246   Window Display Box

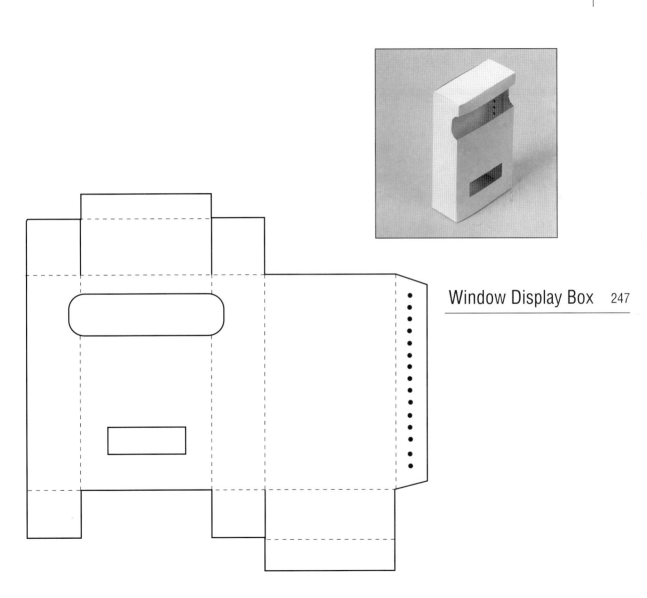

Window Display Box   247

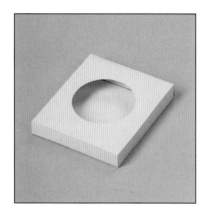

248 Window Display Box

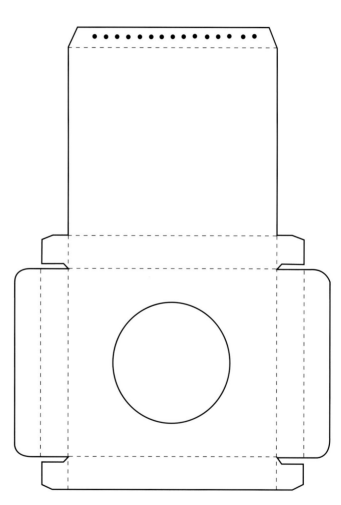

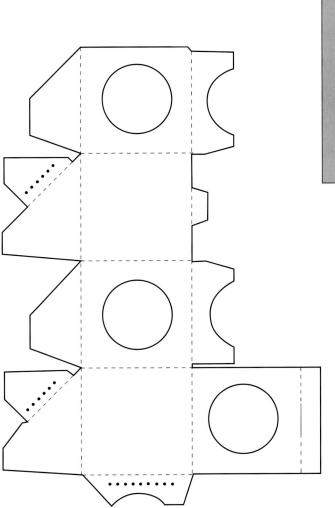

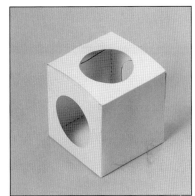

Window Display Box 249

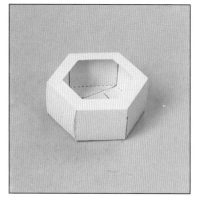

250 **Hexagonal Tray with Window Cover**

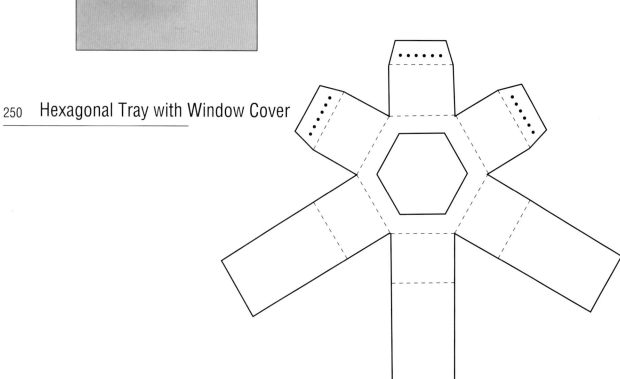

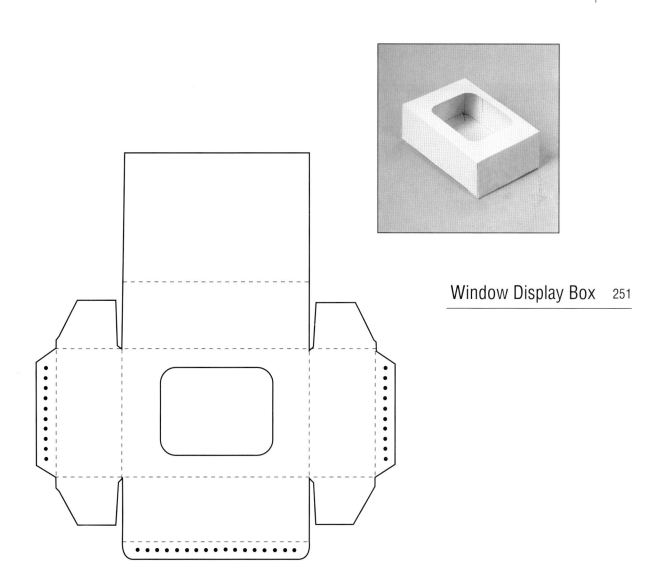

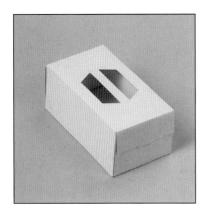

252   Window Display Box

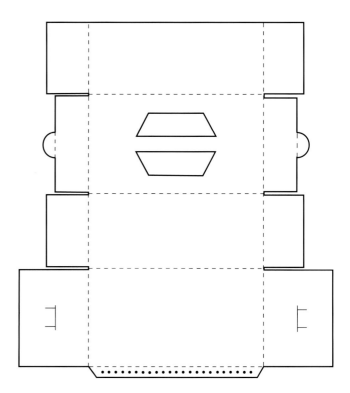

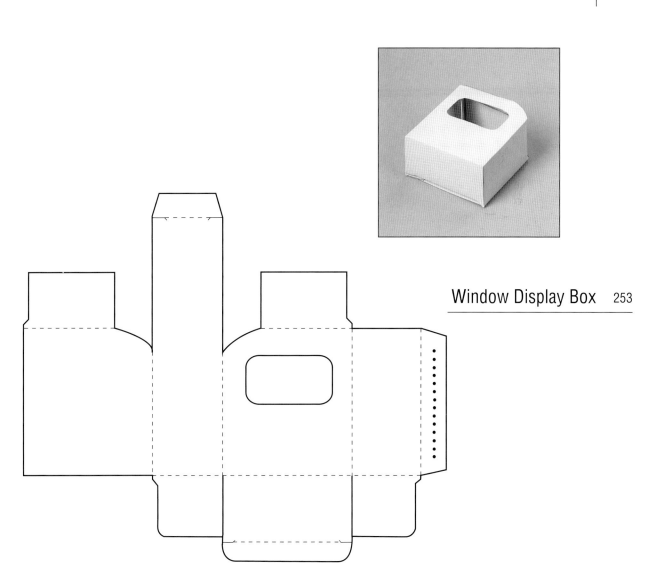

Window Display Box   253

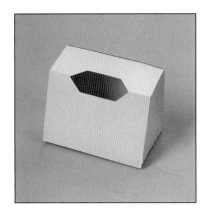

254 Window Display Box

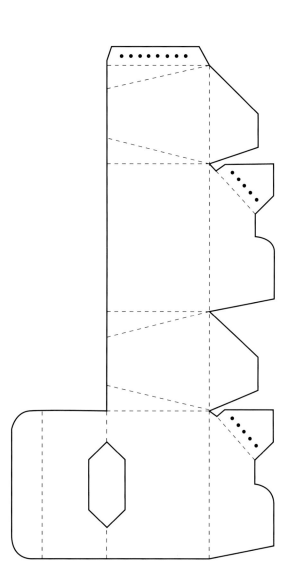

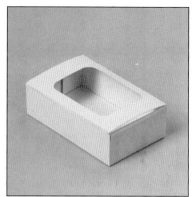

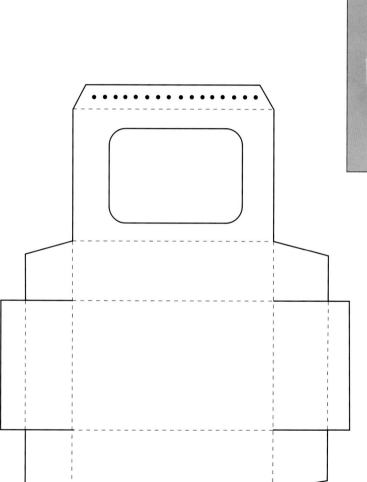

Window Display Box 255

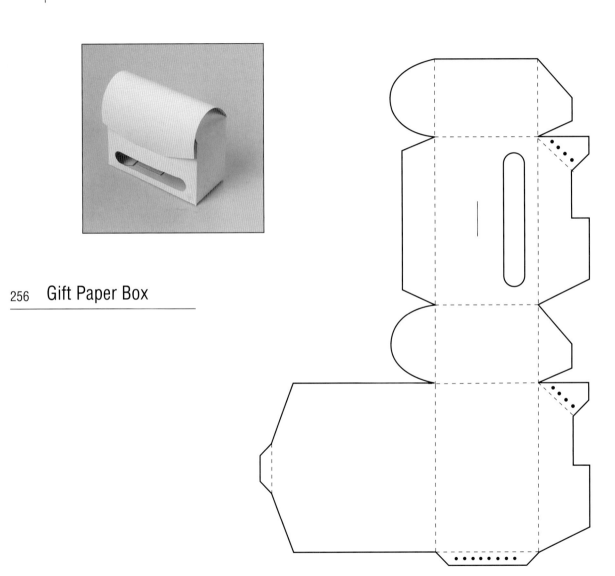

256   Gift Paper Box

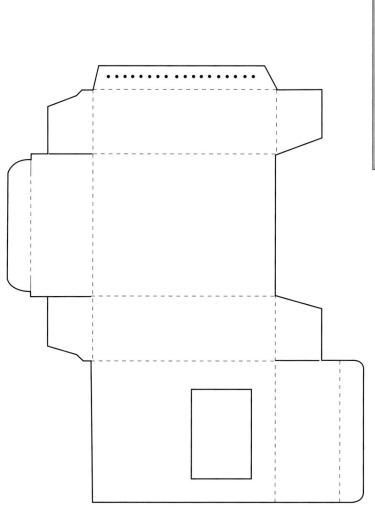

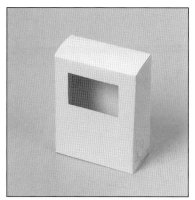

Reverse Tuck Window Box   257

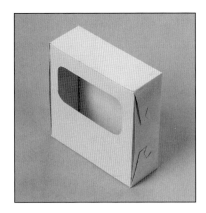

Side-locking Cake Box with Window

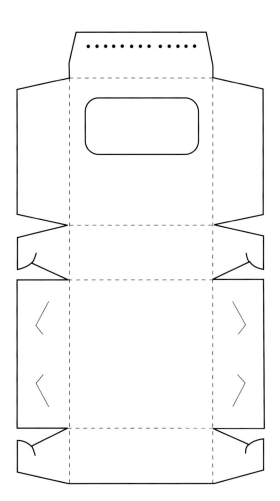

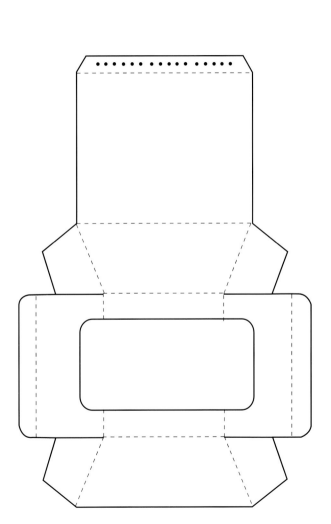

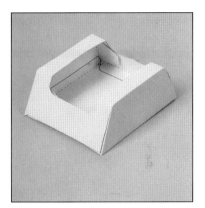

Window Box with Tapered Sides 259

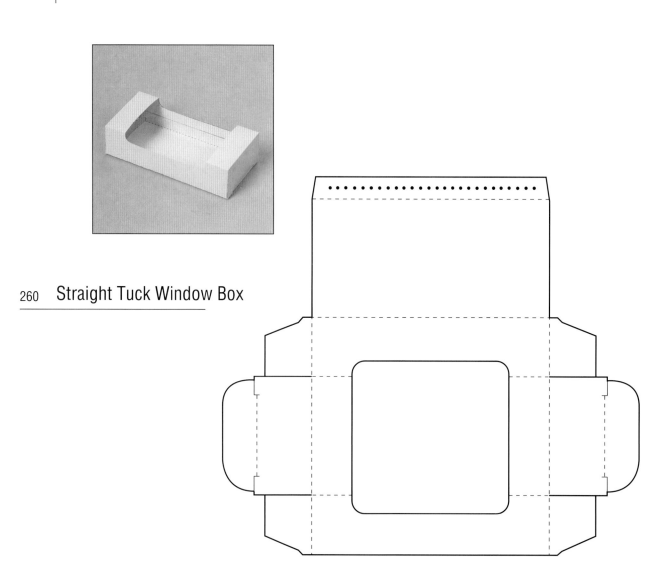

Straight Tuck Window Box

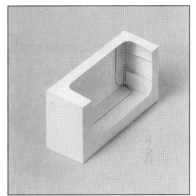

Window Display Box   261

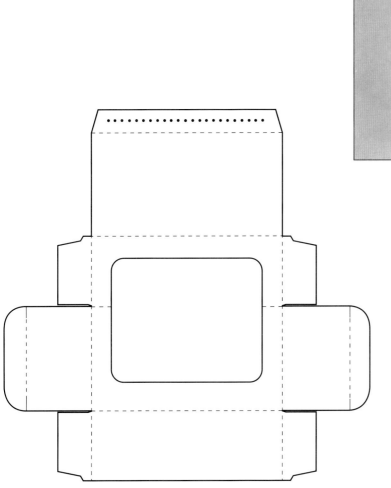

262 Display Box with Window

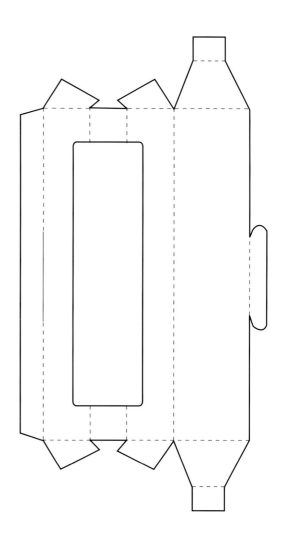

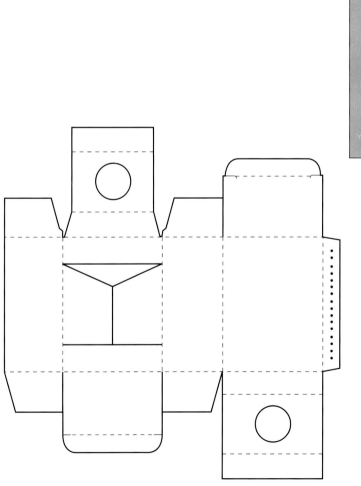

Bottle Display 263

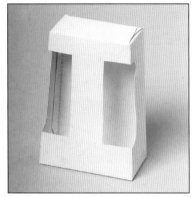

264 Tapered Display Box

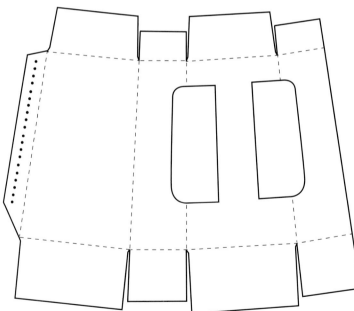

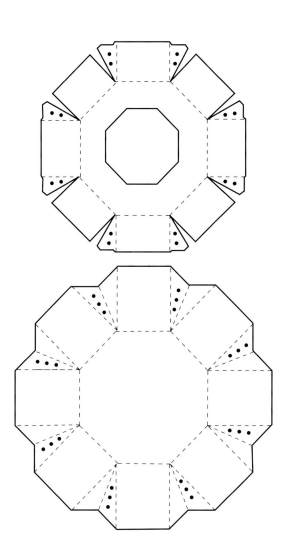

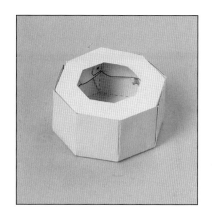

Octagonal Tray with Window Cover 265

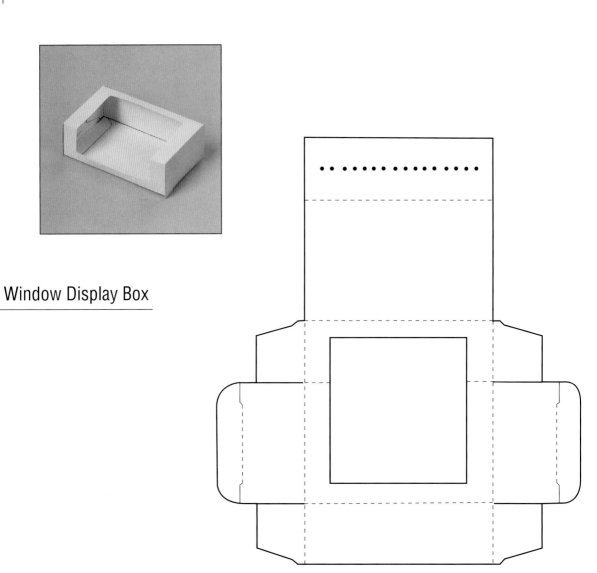

Window Display Box

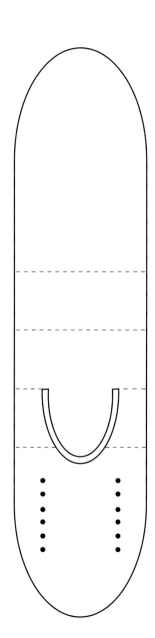

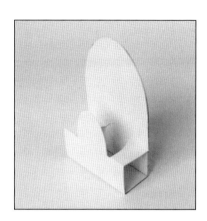

Simple Rack 267

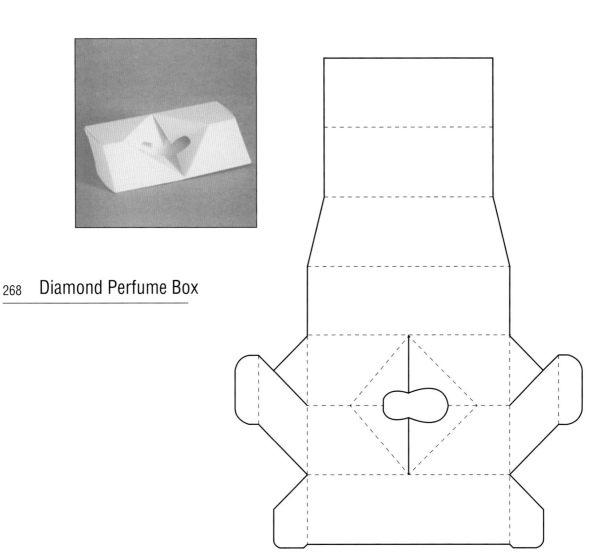

Diamond Perfume Box

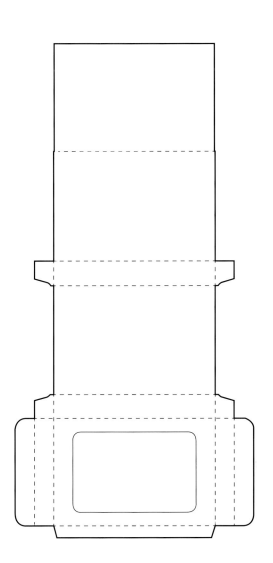

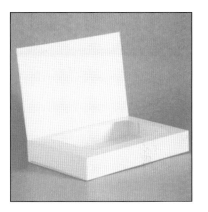

Book-shaped Window Box   269

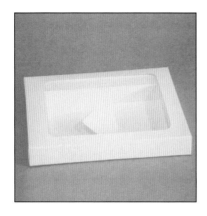

270   S.T.E Window Box

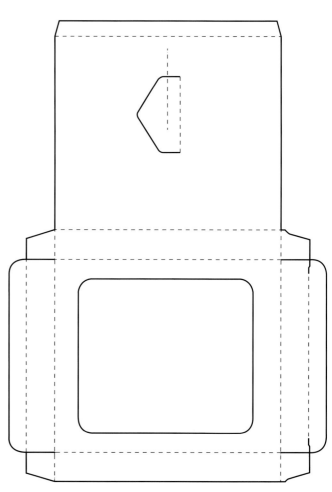

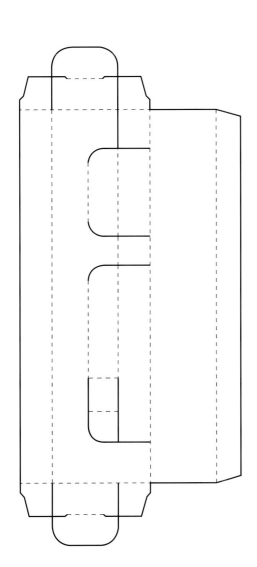

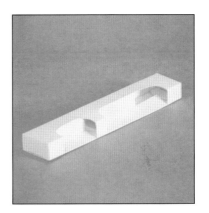

S.T.E Exposed Pen Box   271

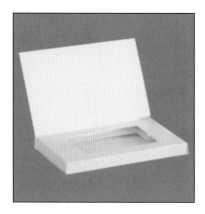

Book-shaped Tape Box

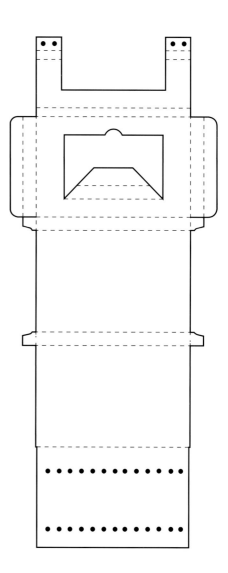

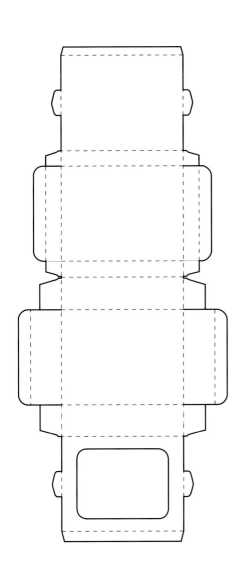

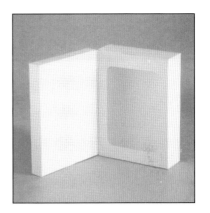

S.T.E Double Book-shaped Box   273

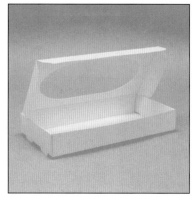

274 **Box with Foot Lock**

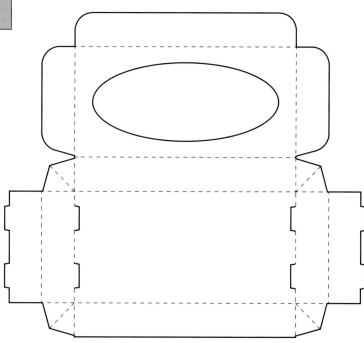

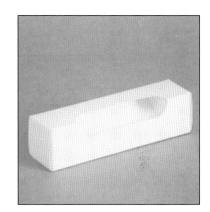

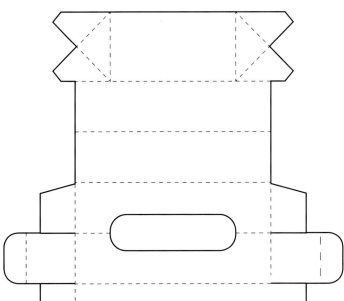

S.T.E Lining 275

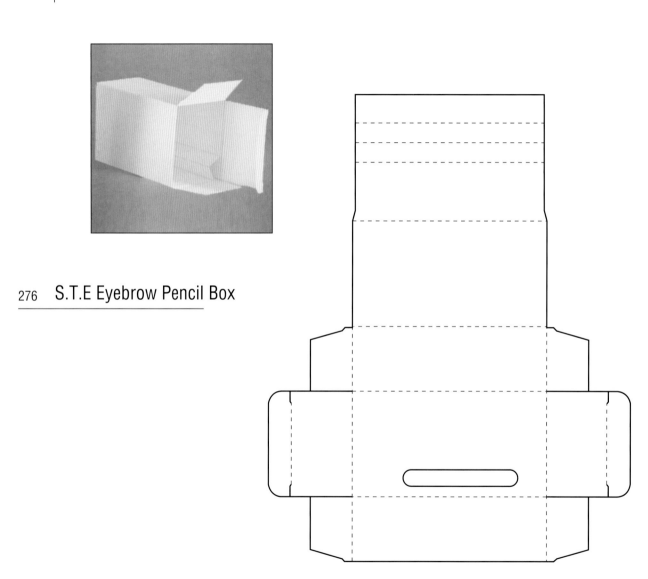

276 S.T.E Eyebrow Pencil Box

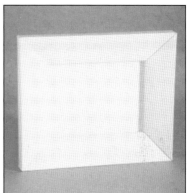

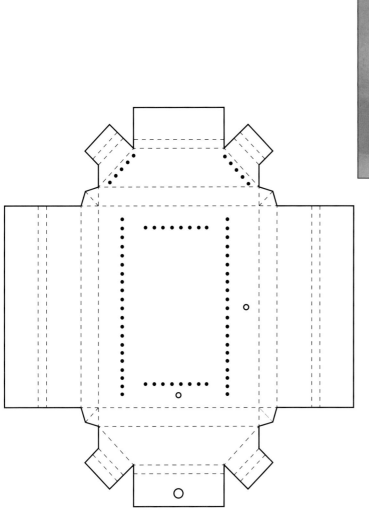

Frame-shaped Box 277

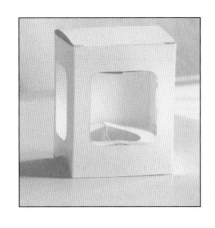

S.T.E Box Top and Bottom Pedestals

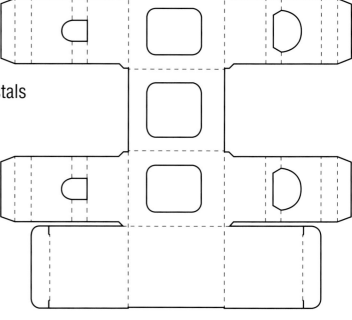

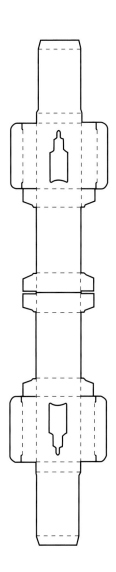

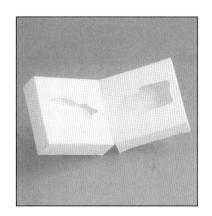

Perfume Display Box   279

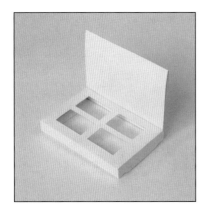

Book-shaped Window Box

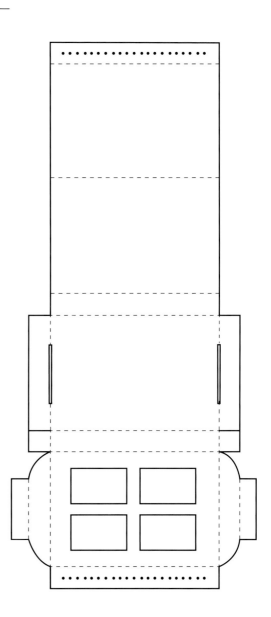

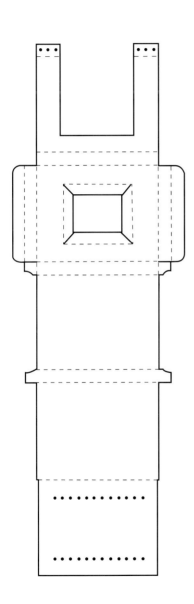

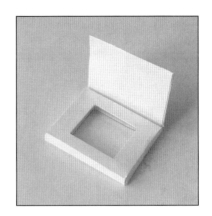

Book-shaped Window Box 281

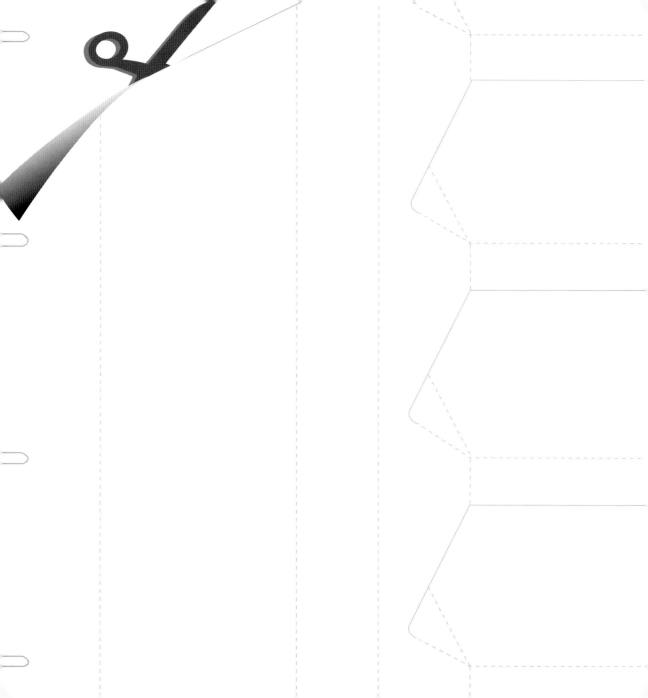

Easel Boxes

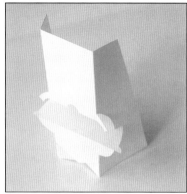

Display Easel

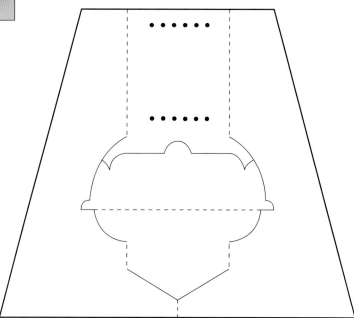

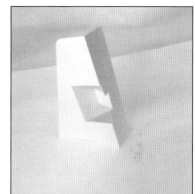

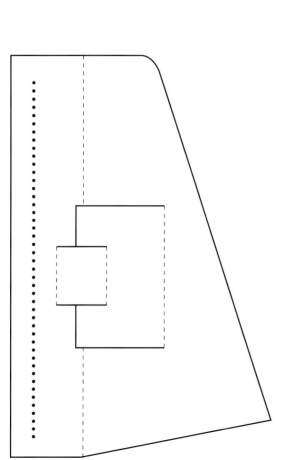

Display Easel   285

Display Easel

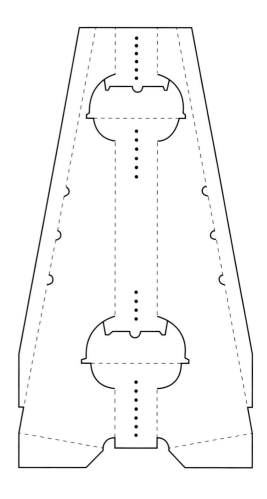

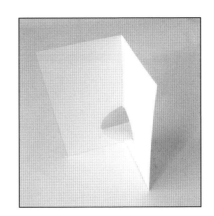

Display Easel   287

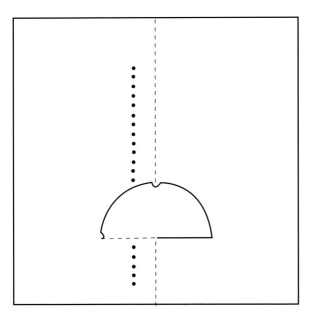

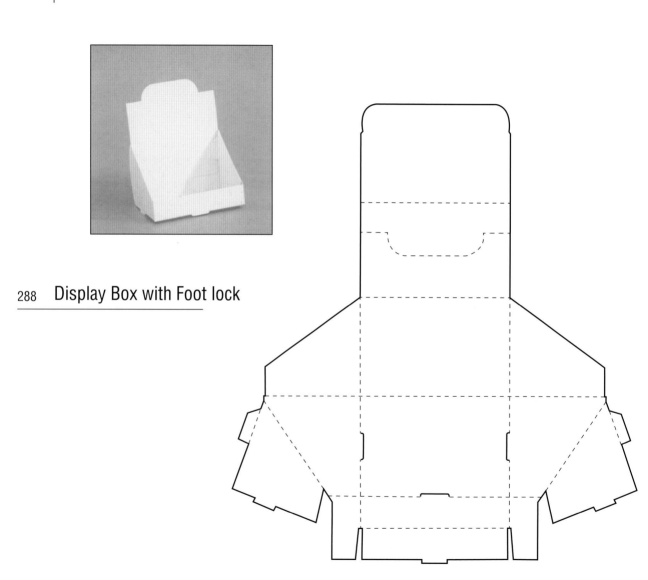

Display Box with Foot lock

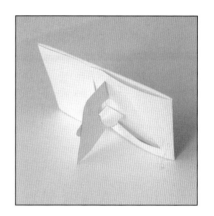

Frame Display Rack   289

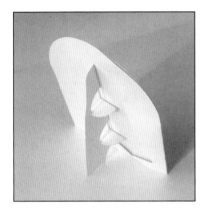

290   Display Tablet with Double Locks

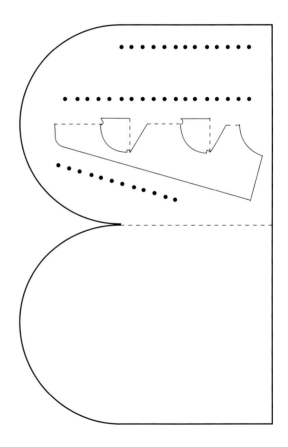

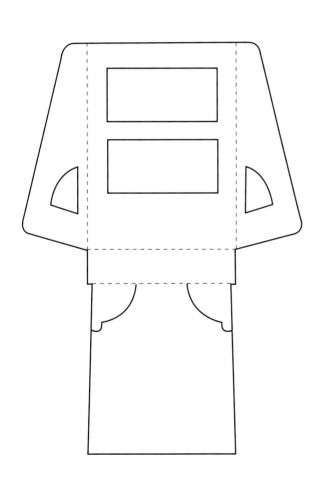

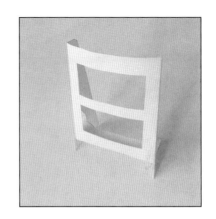

Frame Display Rack 291

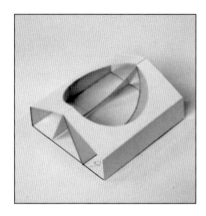

292 **Display Pad**

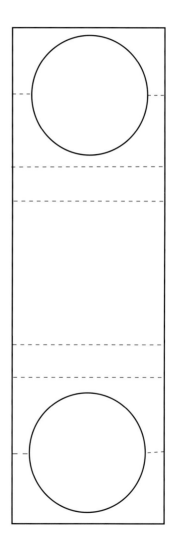

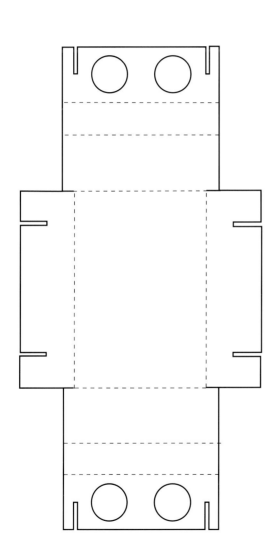

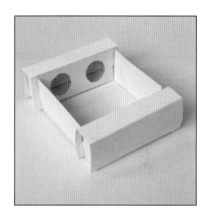

Display Shelf   293

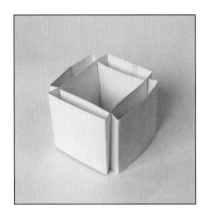

294 Display Shelf

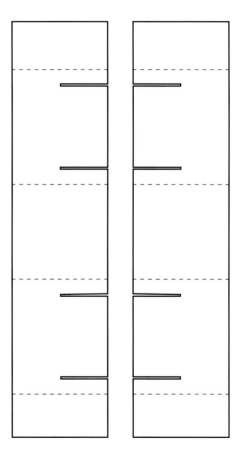

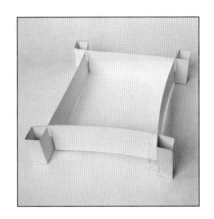

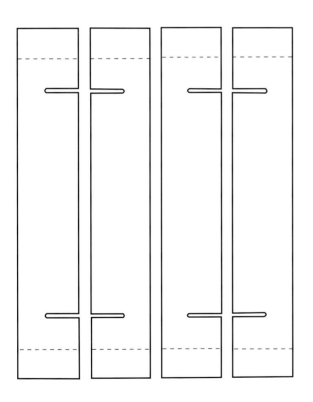

Display Shelf   295

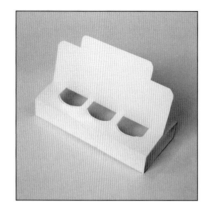

Display Shelf

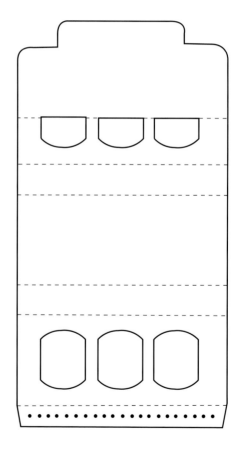

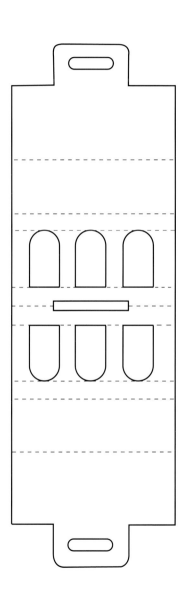

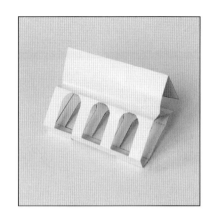

Display Shelf   297

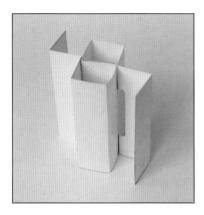

Partitions

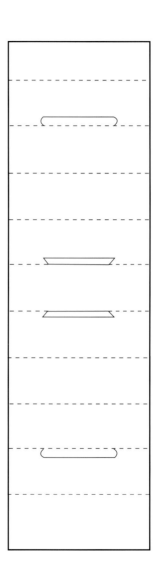

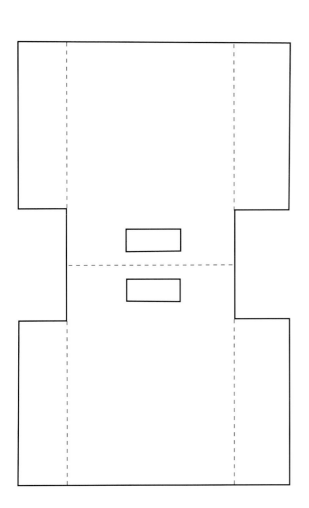

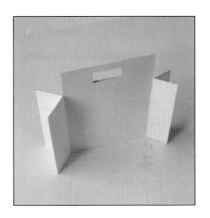

Partitions 299

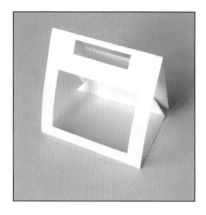

A-Frame Easel

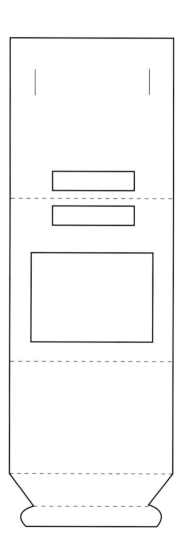

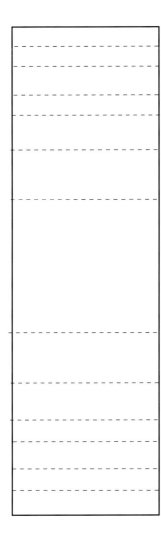

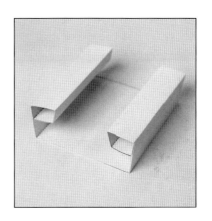

Folded Liners   301

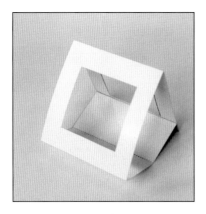

302   A-Frame Easel

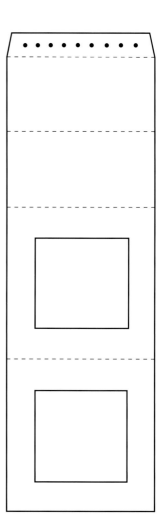

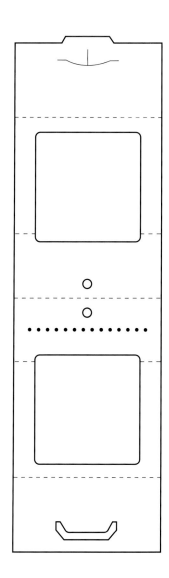

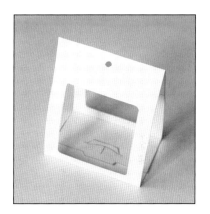

A-Frame Easel 303

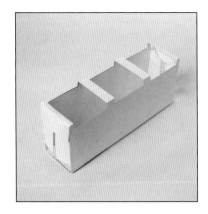

Bottom Lock Display Easel

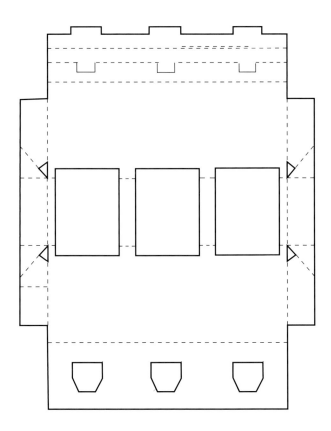

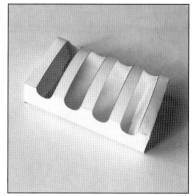

Receding Top and Bottom 305

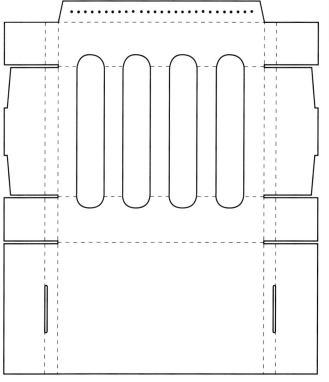

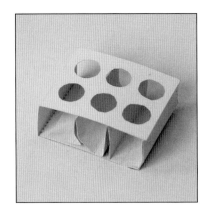

306   Display Shelf

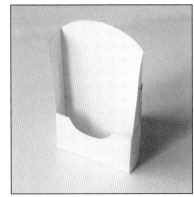

Display Box with Flip Top   307

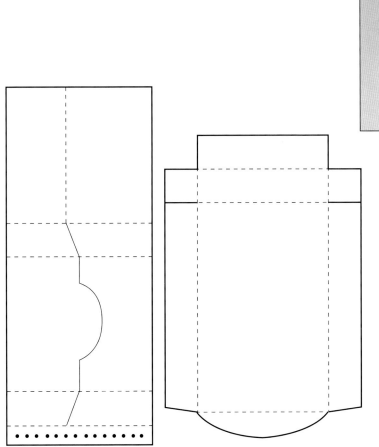

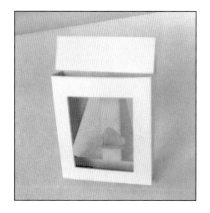

308 Display Rack

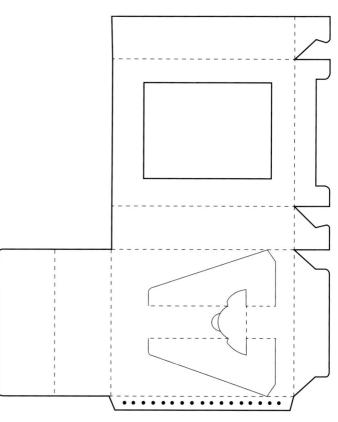

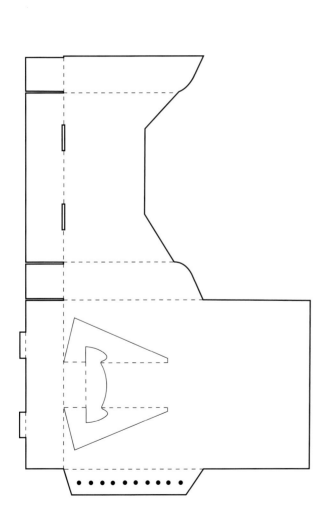

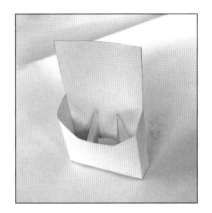

Display Rack 309

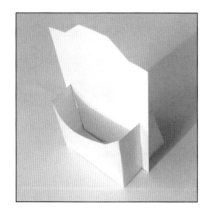

310 Display Rack

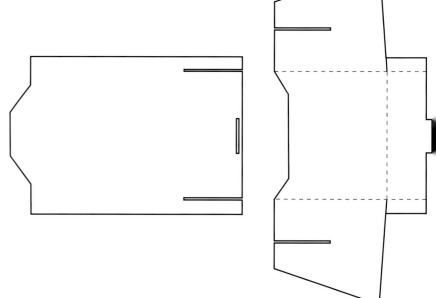

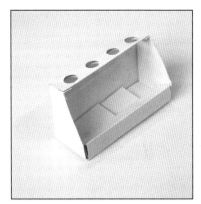

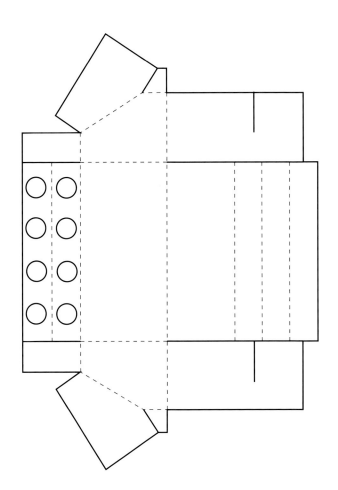

Display Rack   311

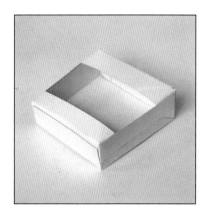

312 Display Rack

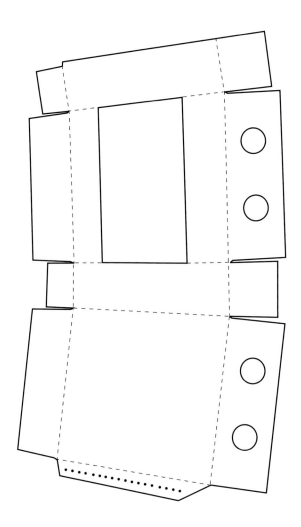

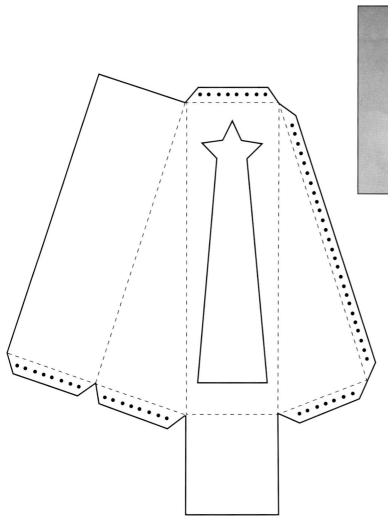

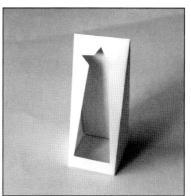

Exhibiting Display Rack   313

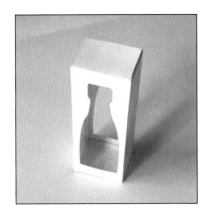

Exhibiting Display Rack

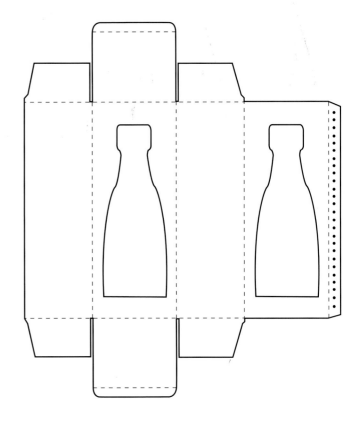

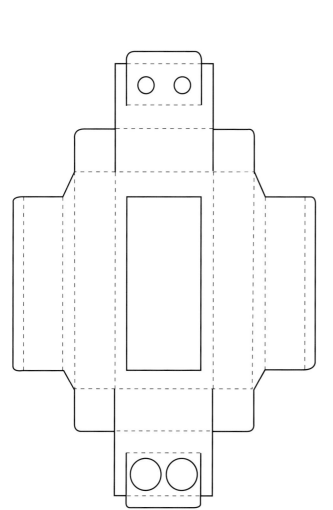

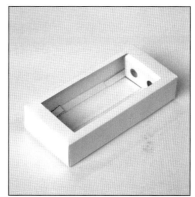

Exhibiting Display Rack   315

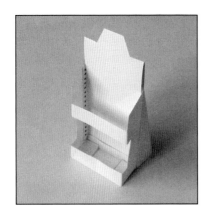

316   Display Rack

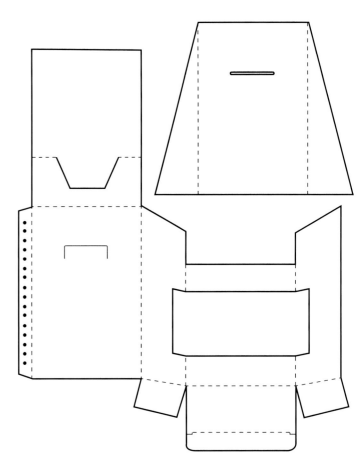

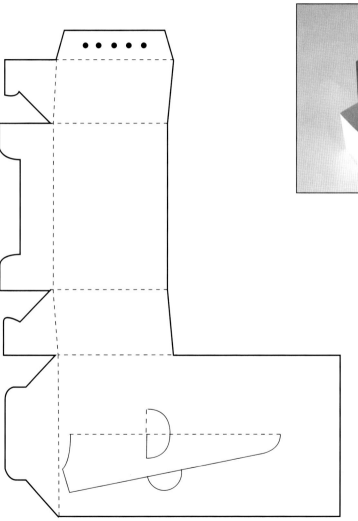

Display Rack 317

318 Frame Display Rack

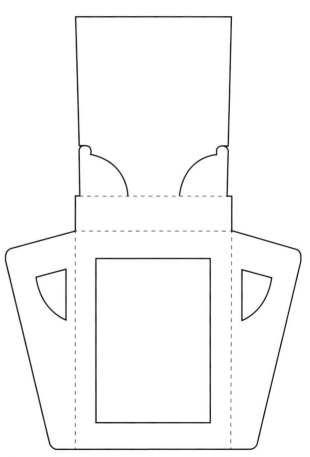

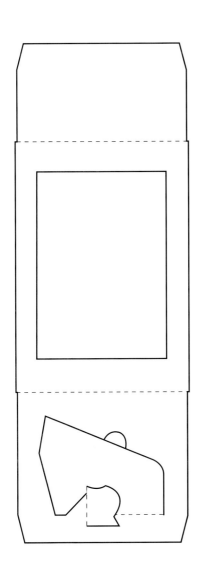

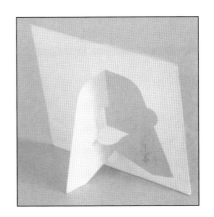

Frame-shaped Display Rack   319

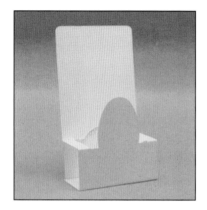

320 **Simple Hanging Box**

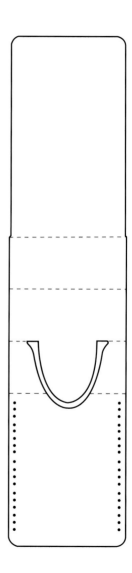

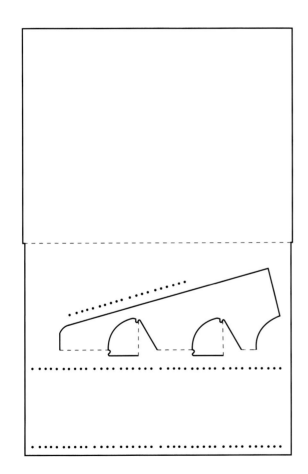

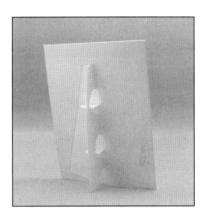

Display Tablet with Double Locks 321

322　Open Display

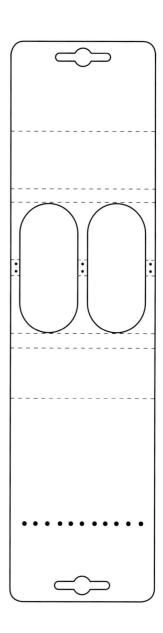

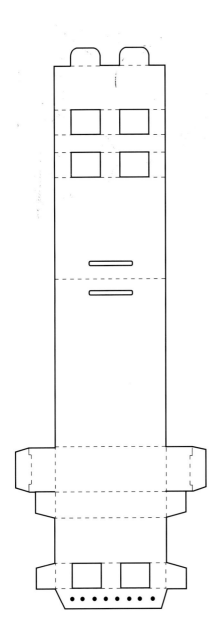

Open Display   323

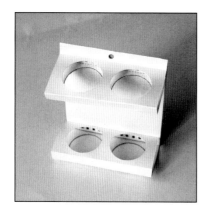

Open Display with Double Back

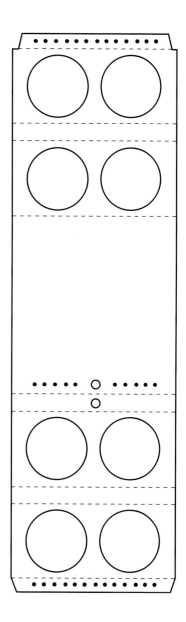

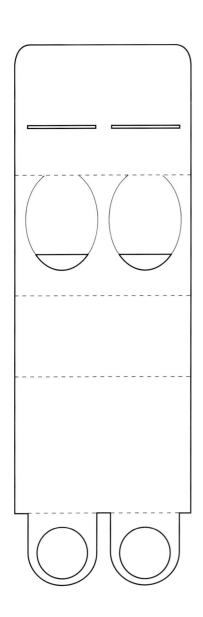

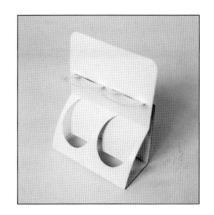

Open Display   325

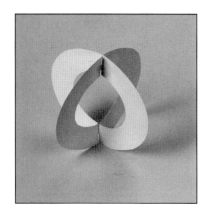

326   Easel Display

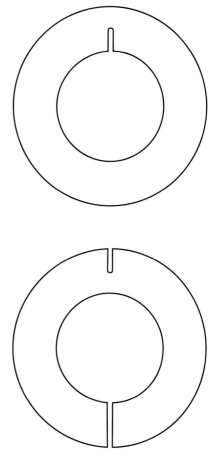

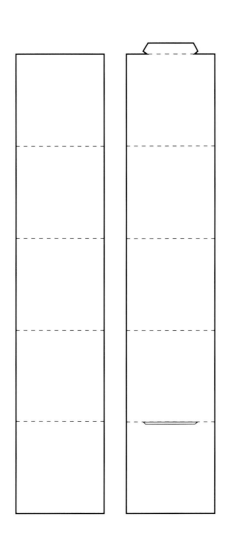

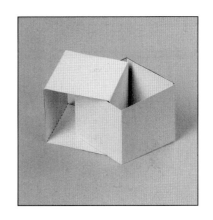

Easel Display   327

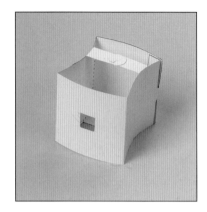

Easel Display

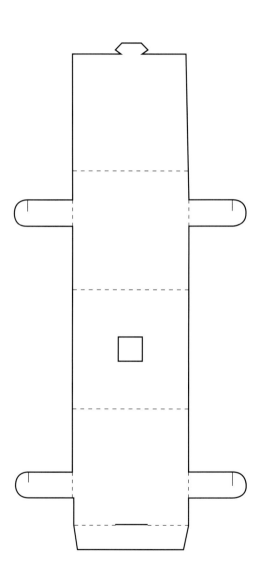

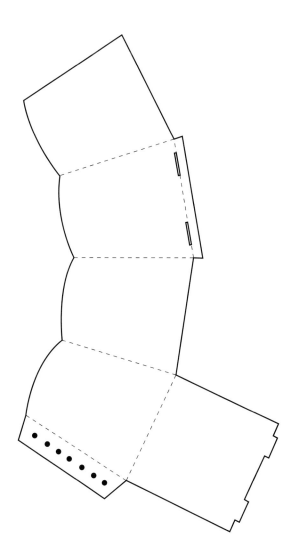

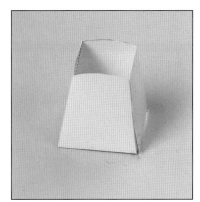

Easel Display 329

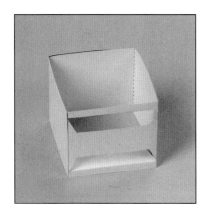

330   **Bellows Easel**

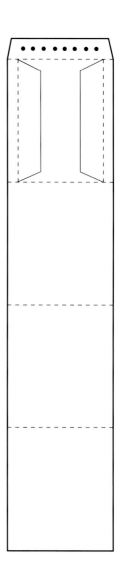

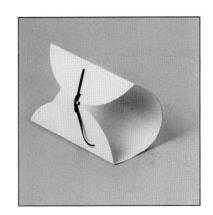

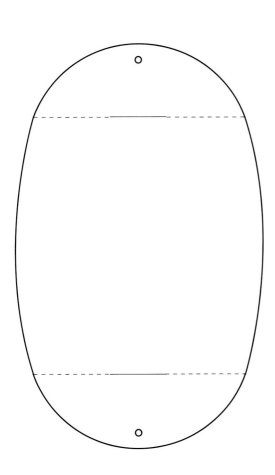

Easel Display   331

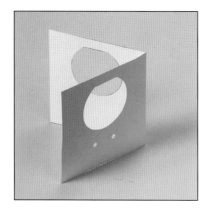

332 Easel Display

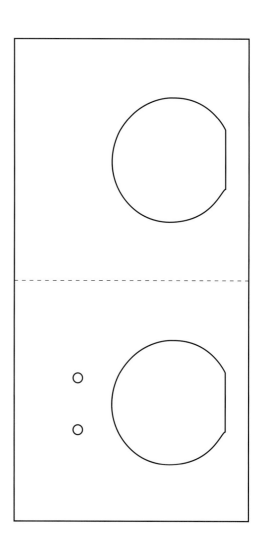

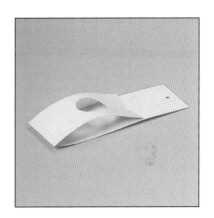

Easel Display 333

334   A-Frame Easel

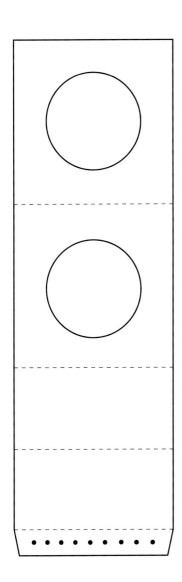

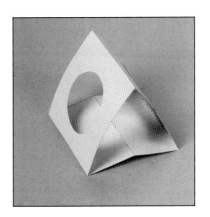

Bellows Easel   335

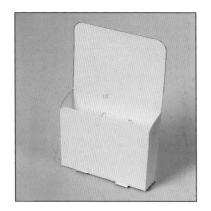

Easel Display

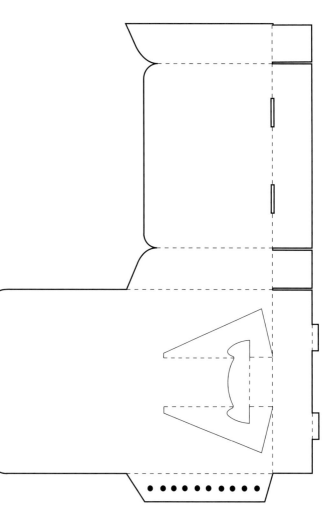

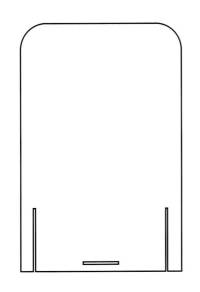

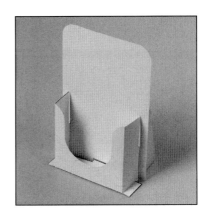

Pocket Easel with Rifle Lock   337

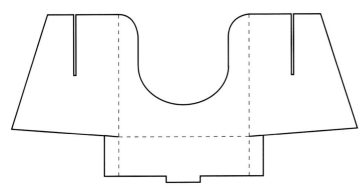

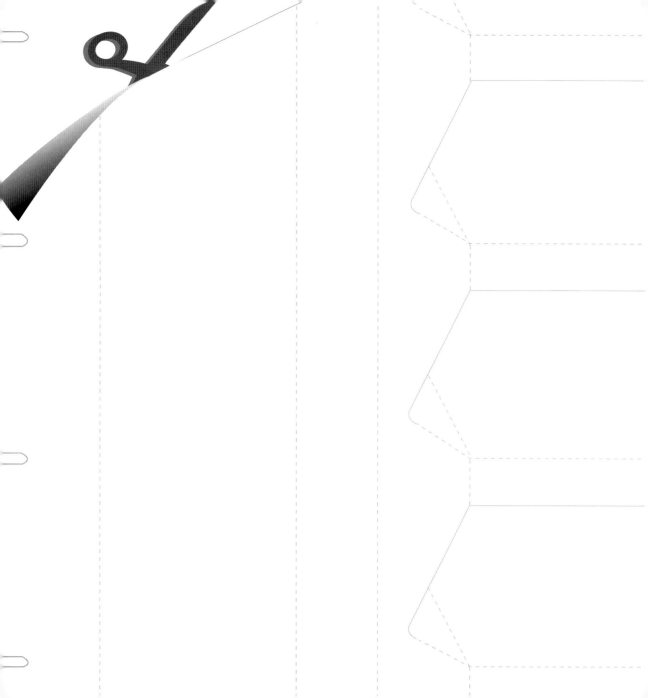

Regular Packaging

340   Box with Click Lock

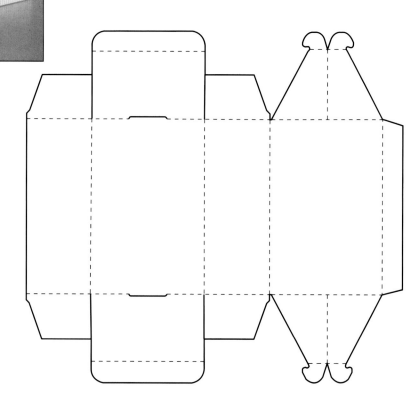

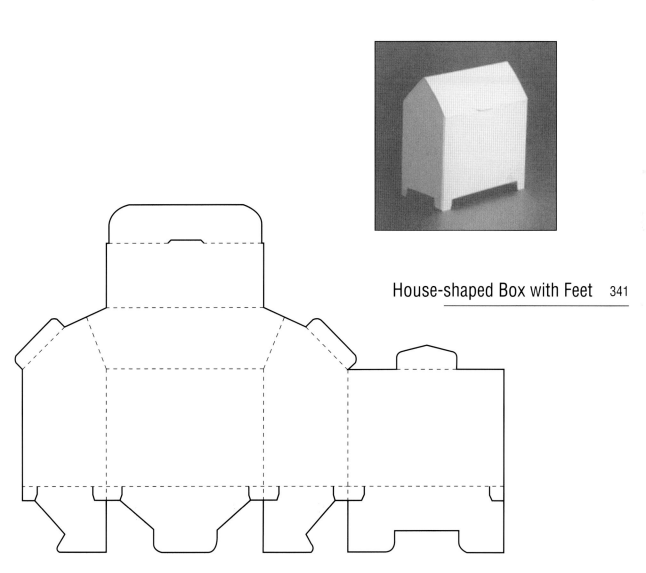

House-shaped Box with Feet 341

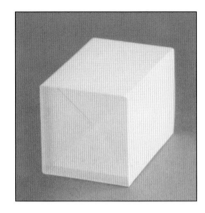

342 Box with Recessed Auto Bottom

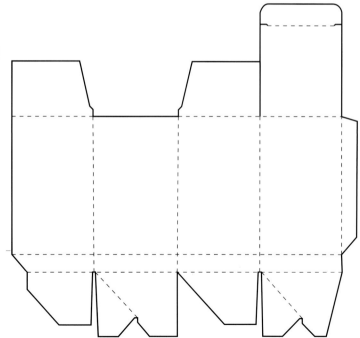

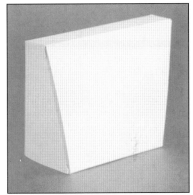

S.T.E.Inclined Box 343

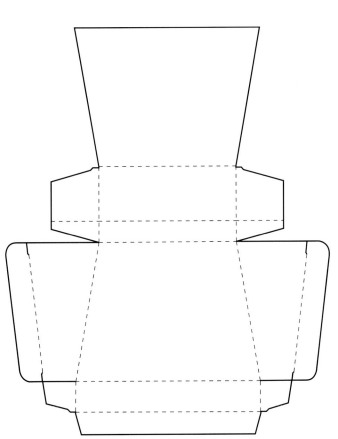

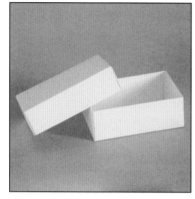

344 Double-walled Box:Lid

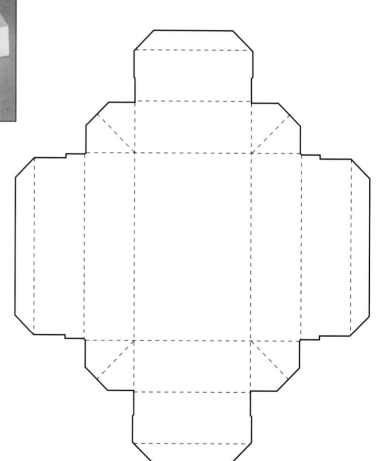

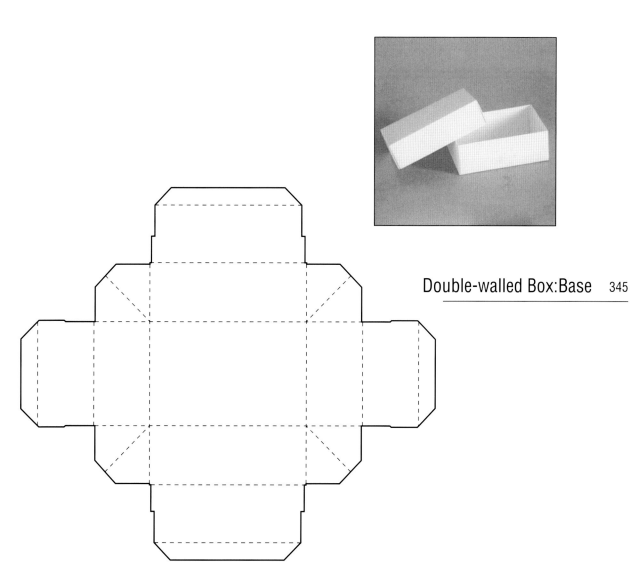

Double-walled Box:Base   345

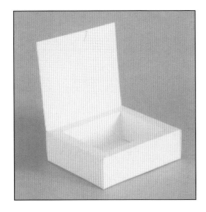

346   Frame-shaped Book Box

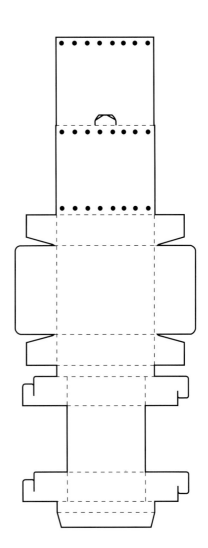

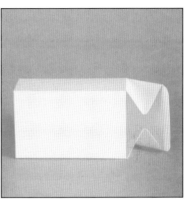

Box with Seamless Top Lid and Auto Bottom 347

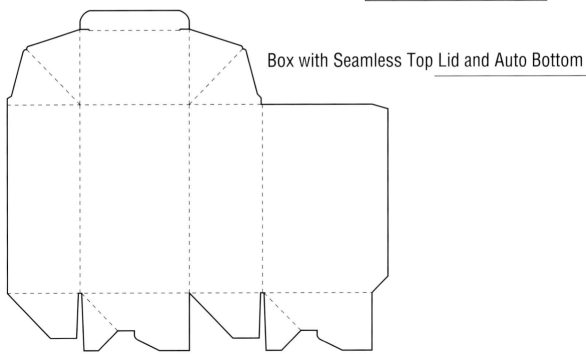

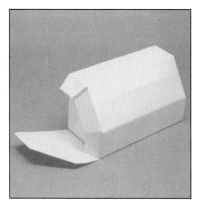

348   Irregular Box with Sealed Ends

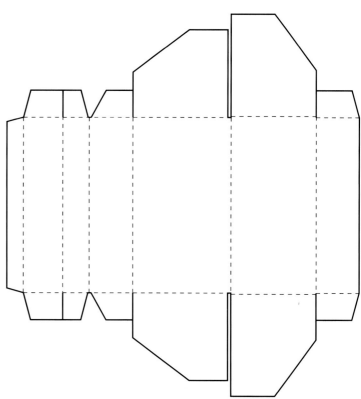

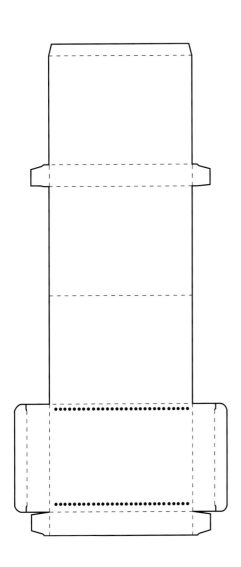

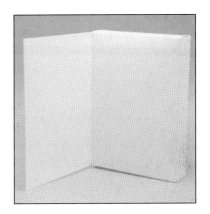

Seamless Book-shaped Box   349

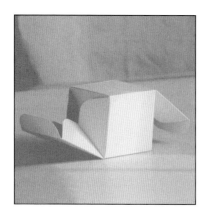

350 R.T.E Seamless Box

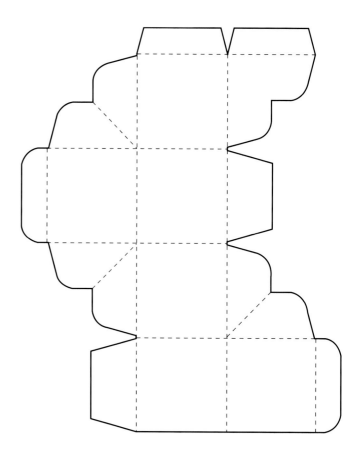

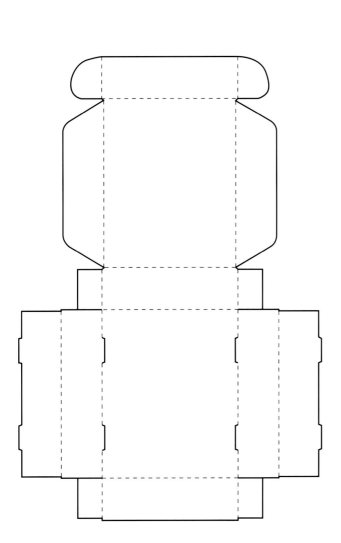

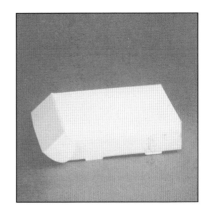

Box with Foot Lock 351

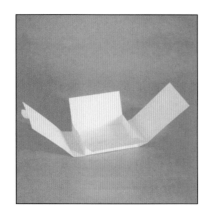

352 Box with Symmetric Double Locks

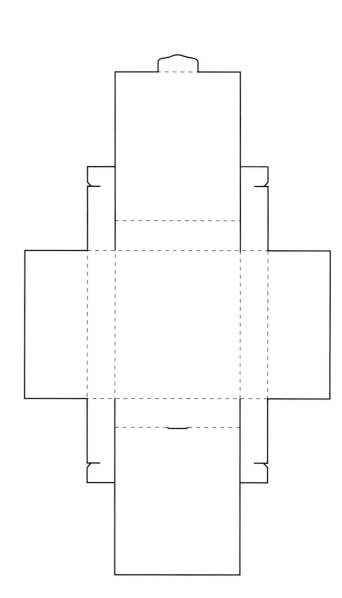

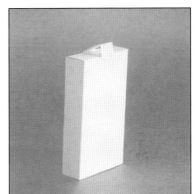

R.T.E Mailbox 353

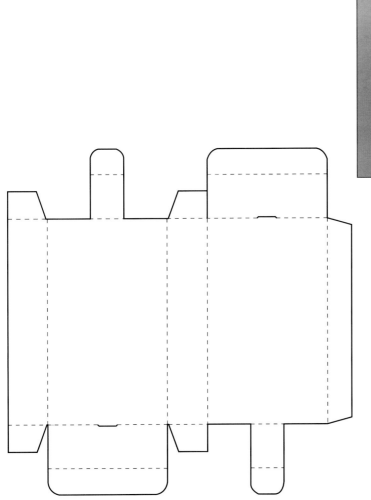

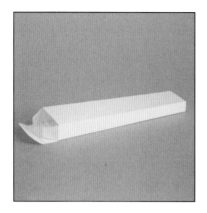

354   S.T.E Trapezoidal Box

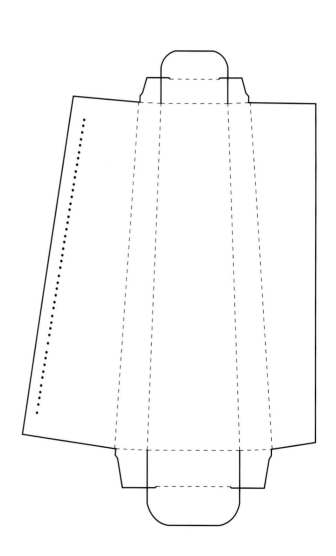

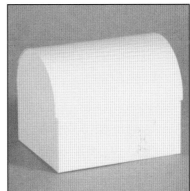

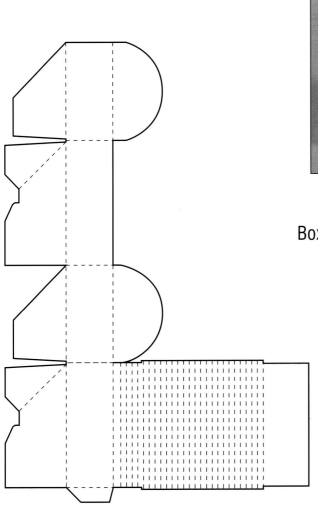

Box with Dome and Auto Bottom   355

356 **Box with Perforated Flip Top**

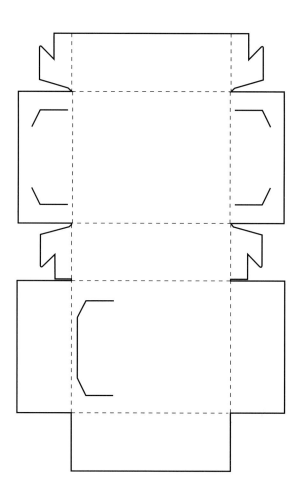

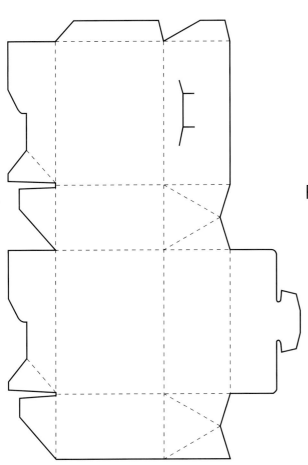

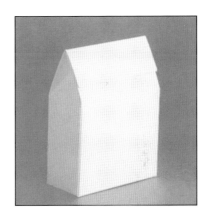

Roof-shaped Top with Outside Lock 357

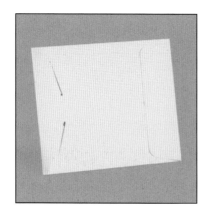

358 Kraft Mailbag

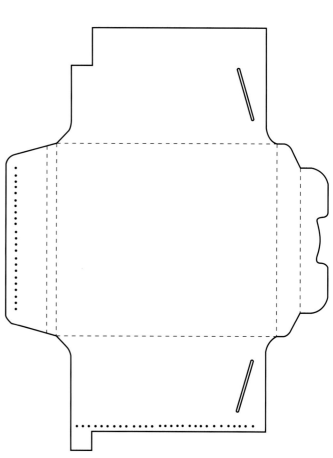

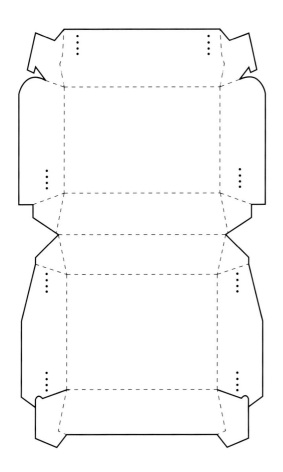

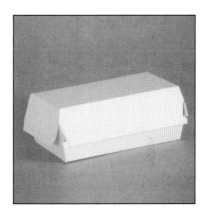

Hamburger Box   359

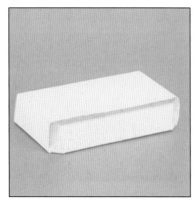

360   Japanese Cake Box

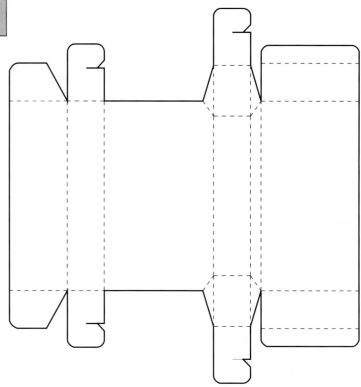

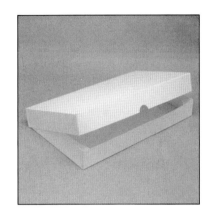

Seafood Takeaway Box 361

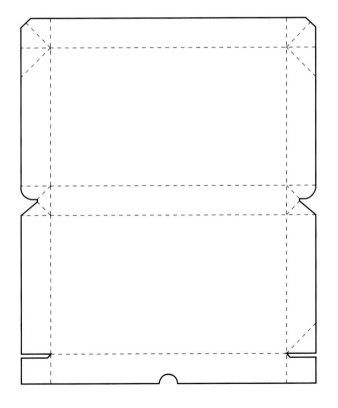

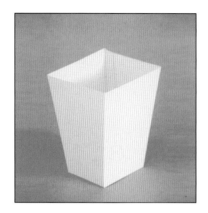

362   Popcorn Box

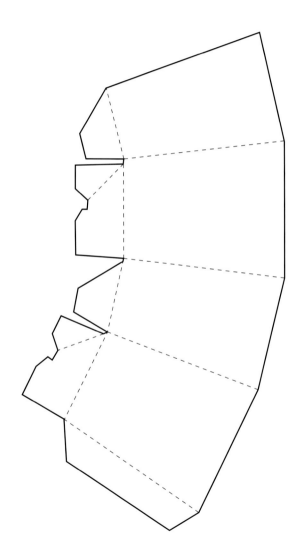

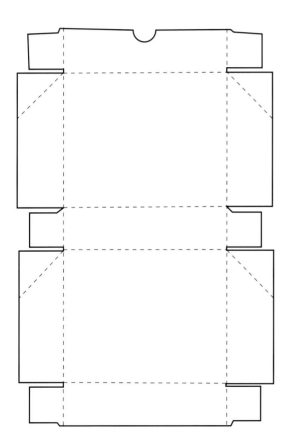

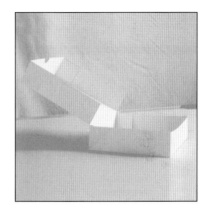

Six-points-glued Box 363

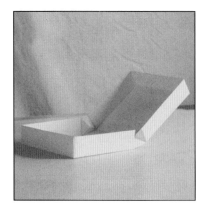

Double-walled-Glued Box

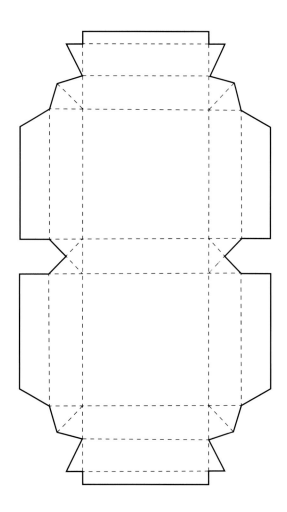

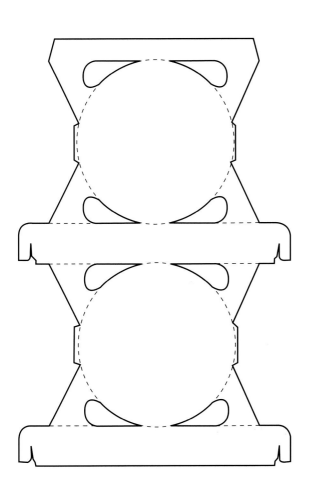

Round Cheese Box 365

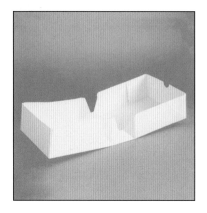

366 Four-points-glued Box

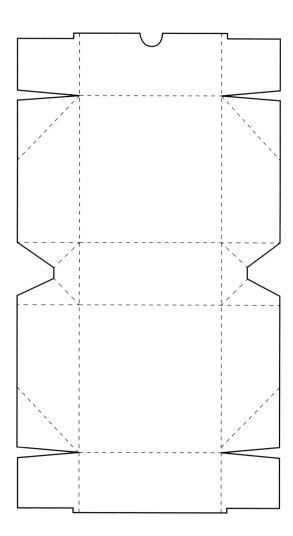

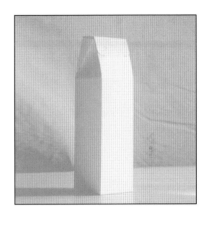

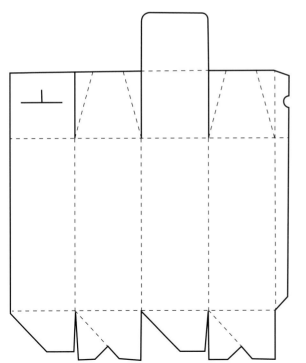

Box with Roof-shaped and Auto Bottom   367

368 Revolved Hexagonal Column Box

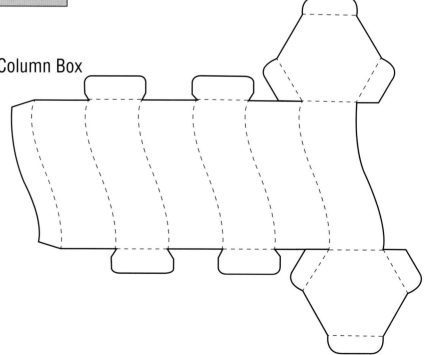

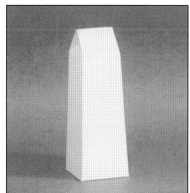

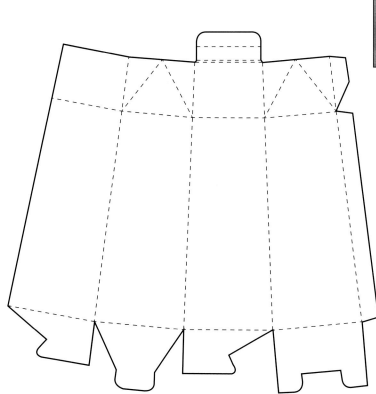

Inclined Tower Box   369

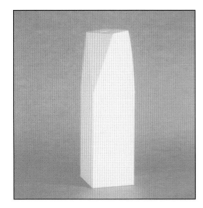

Wine Box with Auto Bottom

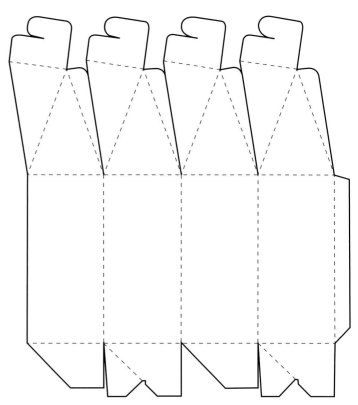

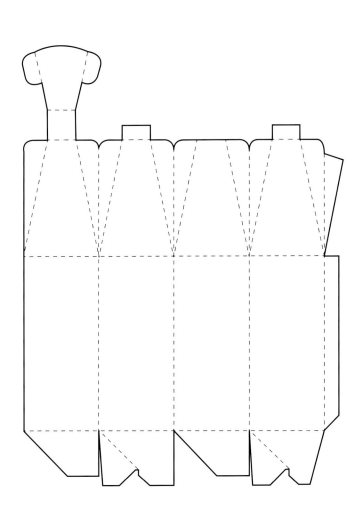

Wine Box with Auto Bottom   371

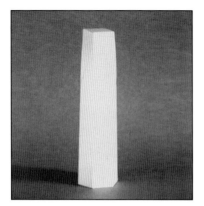

Hexagonal Wine Box with Auto Bottom

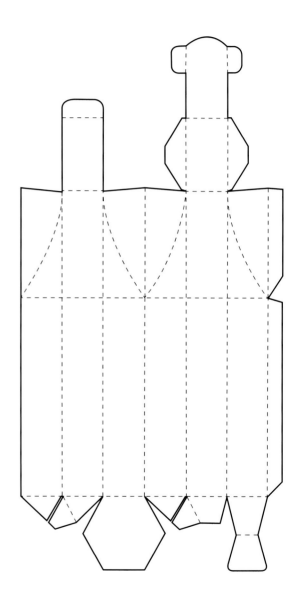

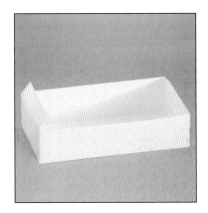

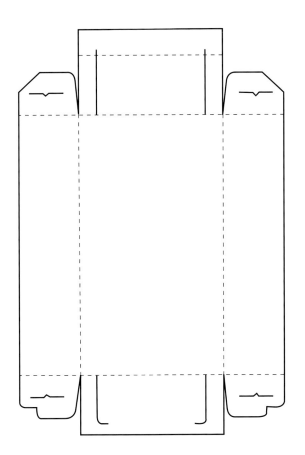

Box with Mini Lock 373

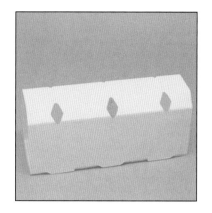

Box with Triple Click Locks

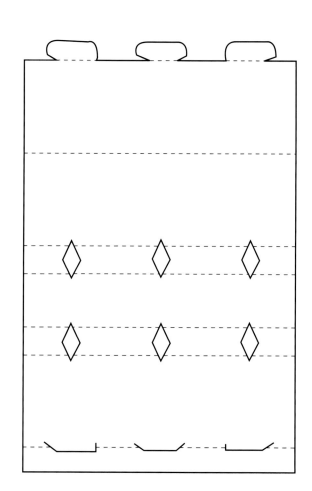

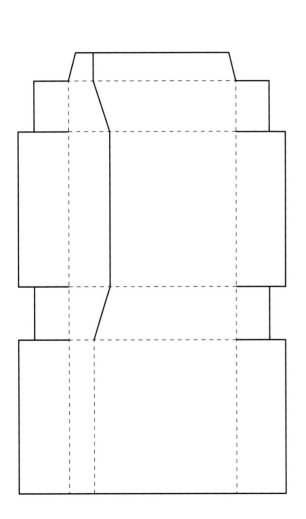

Simple Cigarette Box   375

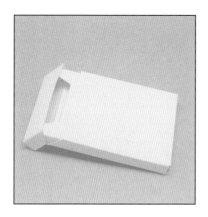

Cigarette Box

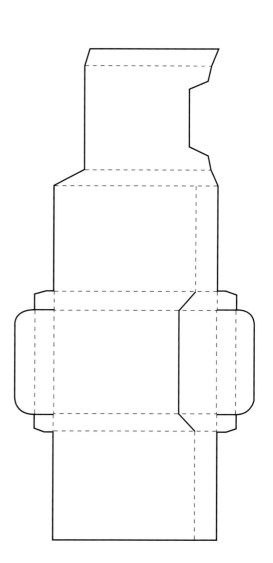

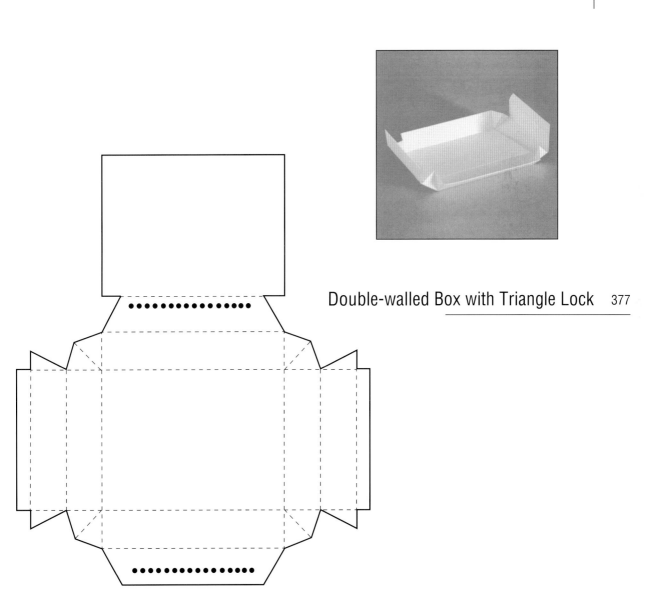

Double-walled Box with Triangle Lock 377

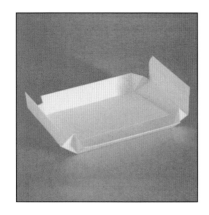

Double-walled Box with Triangle Lock

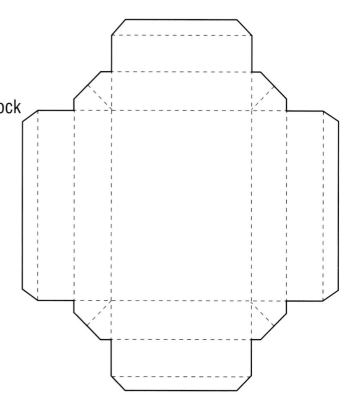

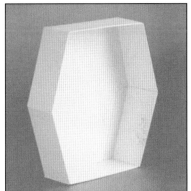

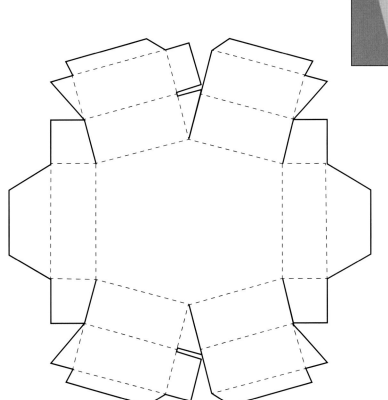

Long Hexagonal Box 379

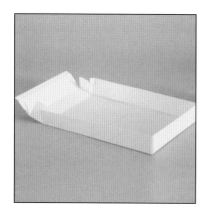

380 **Double-walled Box**

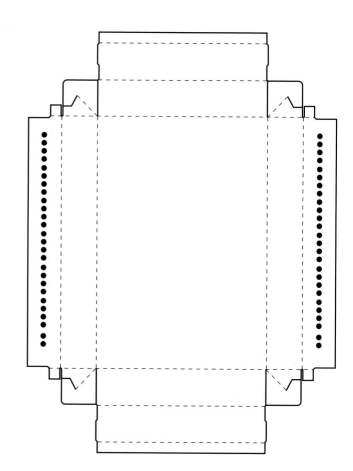

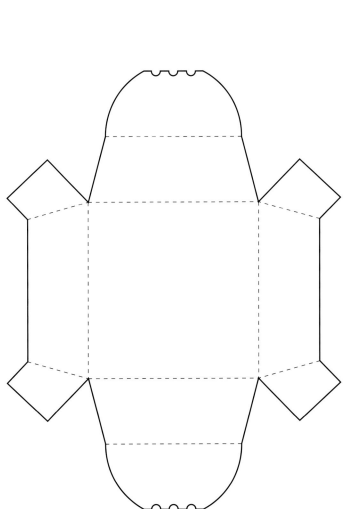

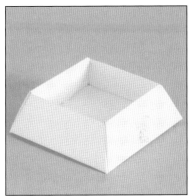

Disposable Dispenser 381

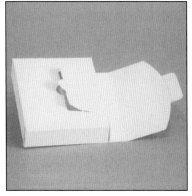

Box with 123 Bottom

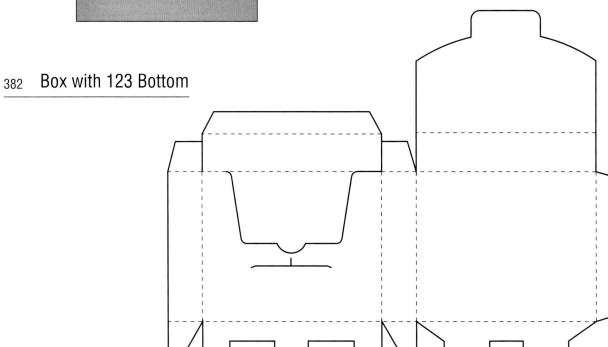

Dispenser 383

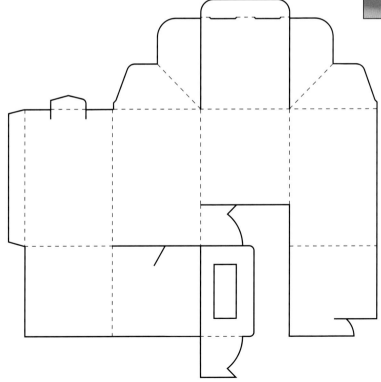

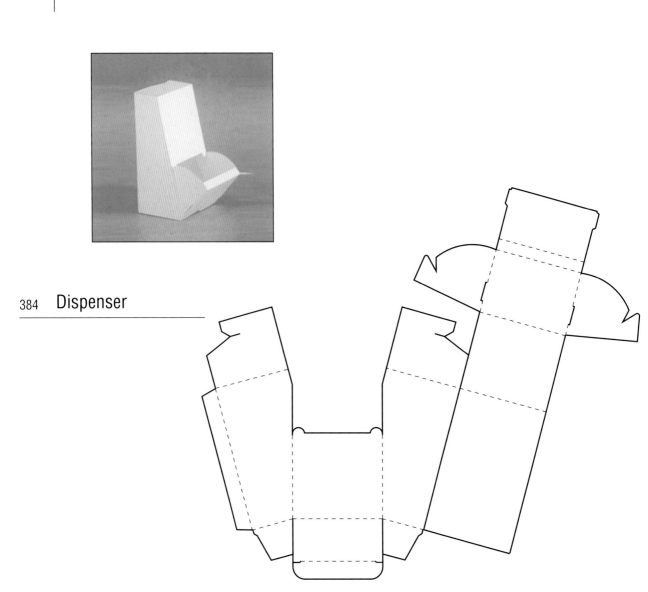

384 Dispenser

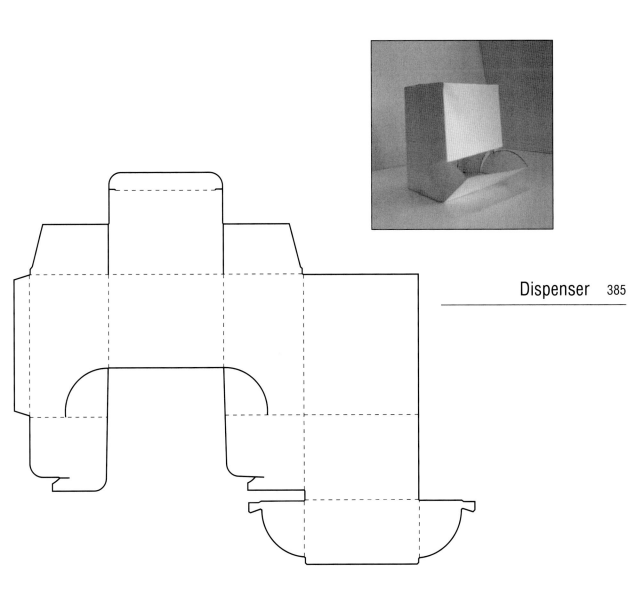

Dispenser 385

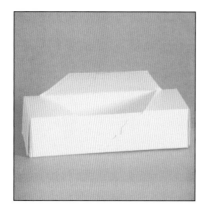

386 Roll Dispenser

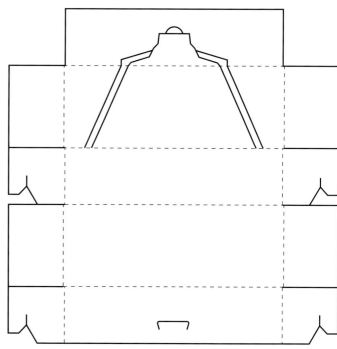

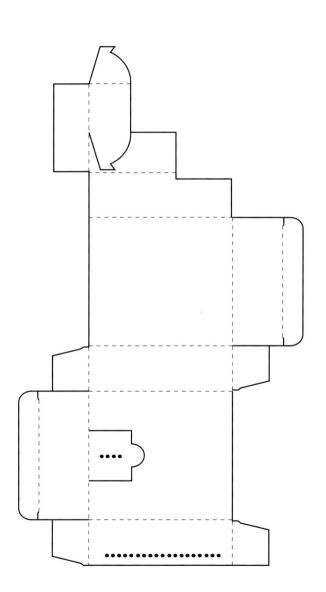

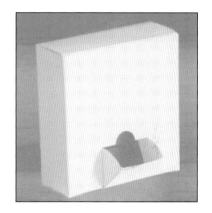

R.T.E.Dispenser 387

Three Panel Double CD Folder

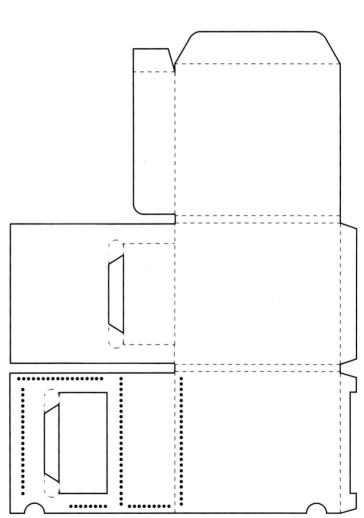

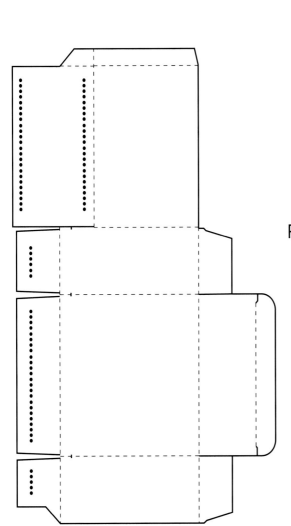

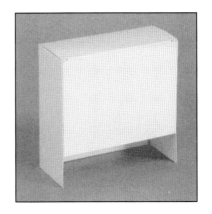

R.T.E CD Box with Reinforced Top Lid   389

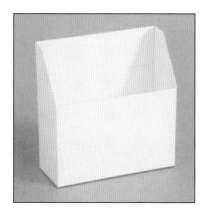

390 CD Box with Reinforced 123 Bottom

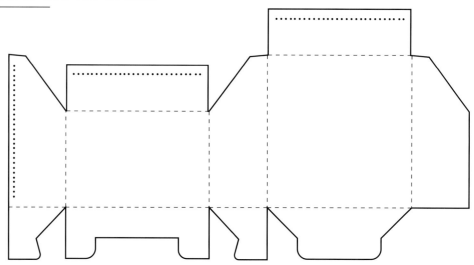

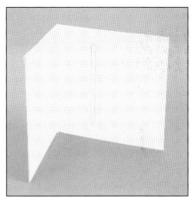

Double-faced CD Folder 391

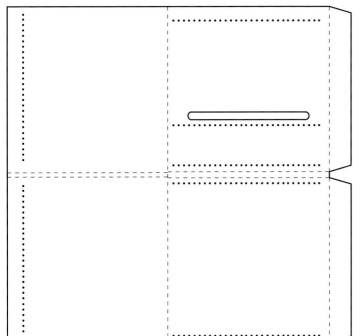

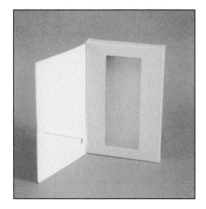

392   Book-shaped Window Box with CD Holder

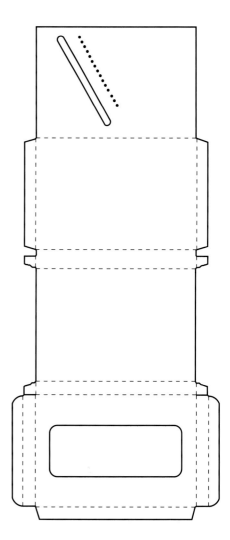

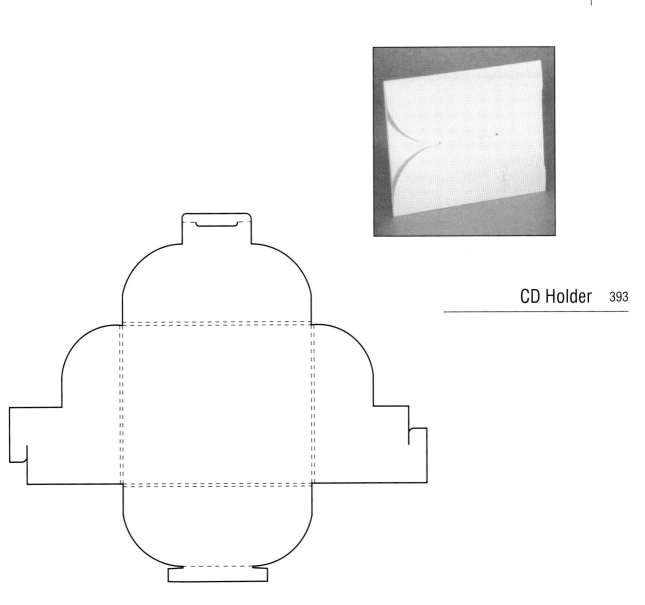

CD Holder   393

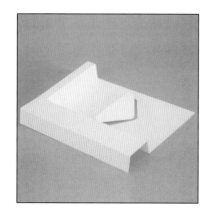

394   CD Lining Holder

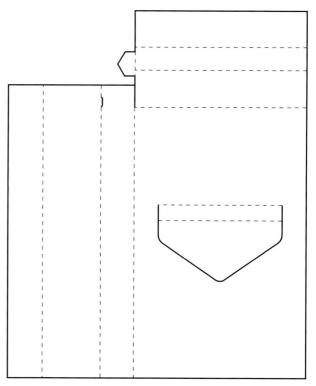

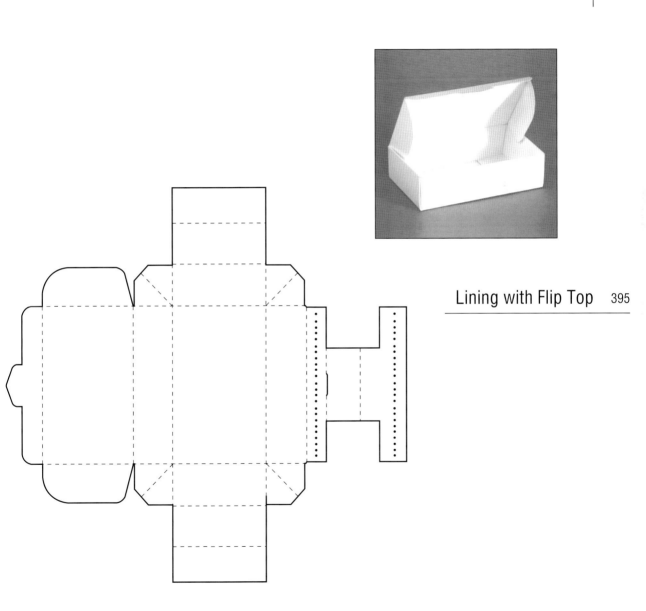

Lining with Flip Top   395

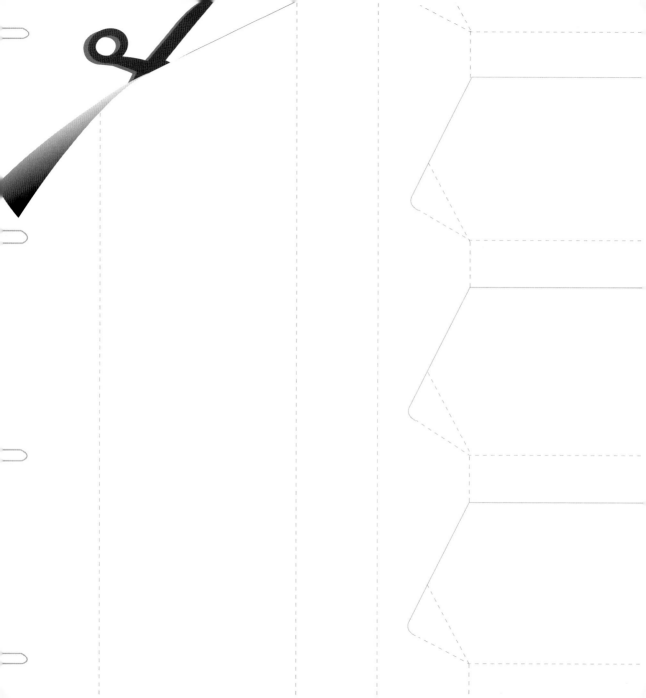

Dividers

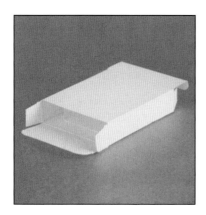

398 R.T.E.Lining Box

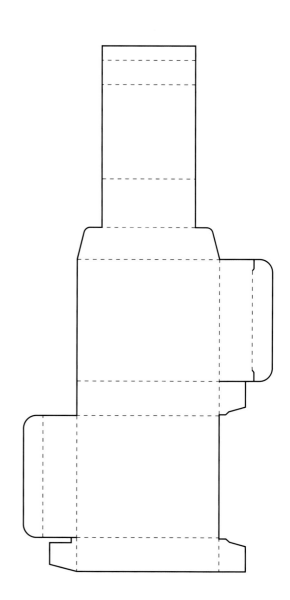

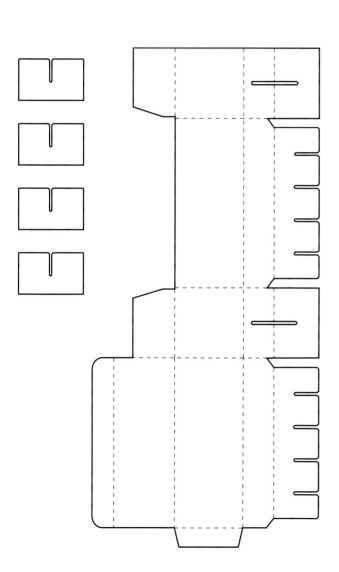

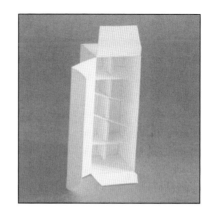

Ten Cell Box 399

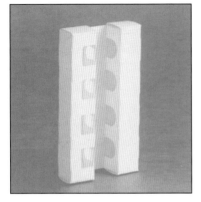

400   Four Cell Divider

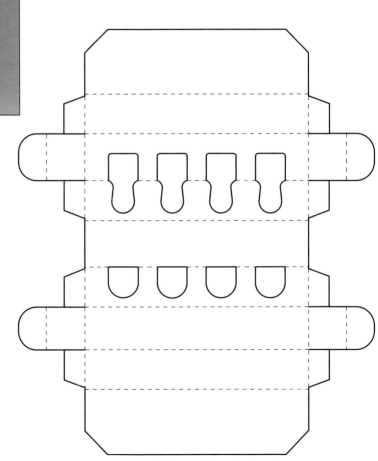

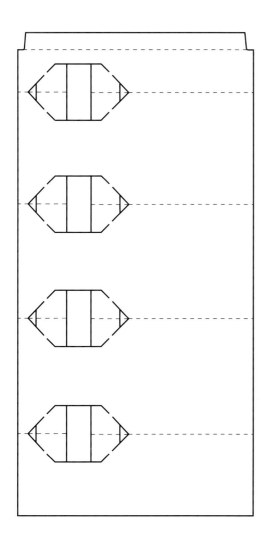

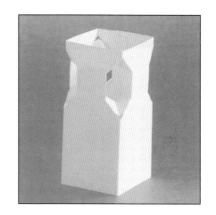

Four Cell Divider   401

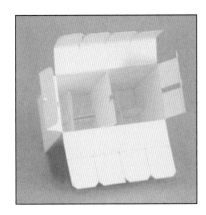

One Piece Eight Cell Box

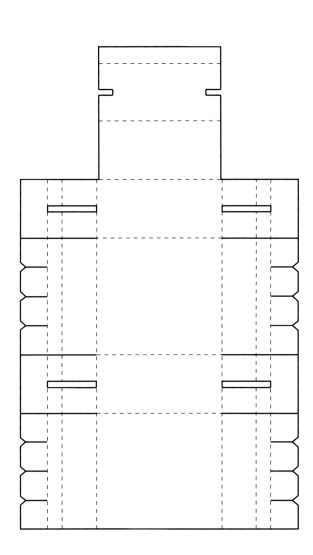

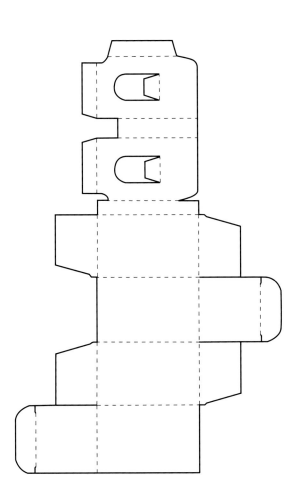

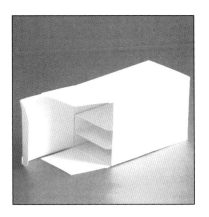

R.T.E.Lining Box   403

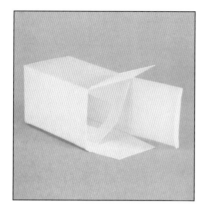

404 R.T.E Diagonal Lining Box

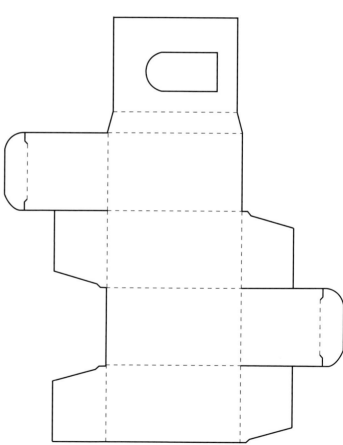

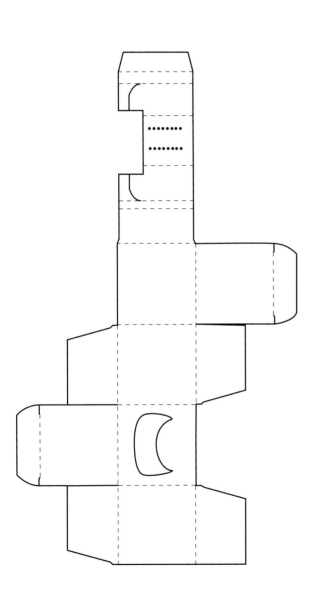

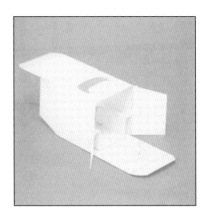

R.T.E. French Lining Box   405

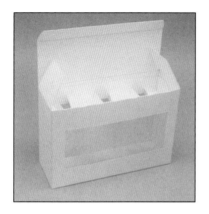

406 One Piece Three Cell Box with Auto Bottom

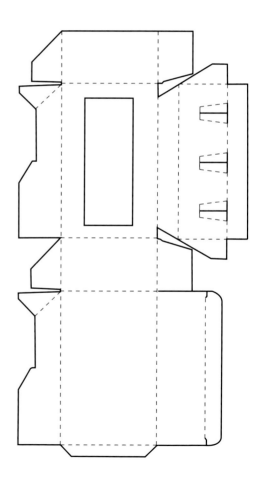

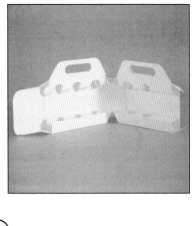

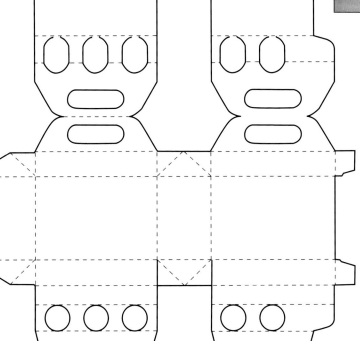

One Piece Five Cell Carrier 407

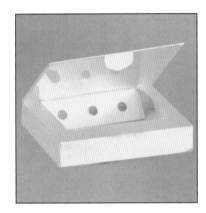

One Piece Three Cell Book-shaped Box

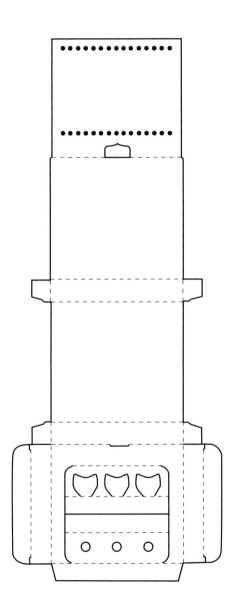

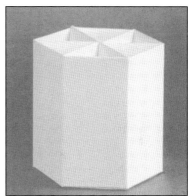

Hexagonal Star Box 409

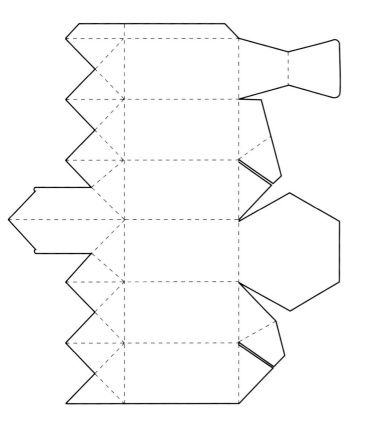

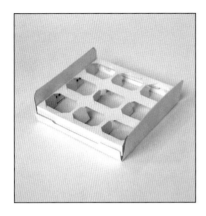

410 Divided Counter Display

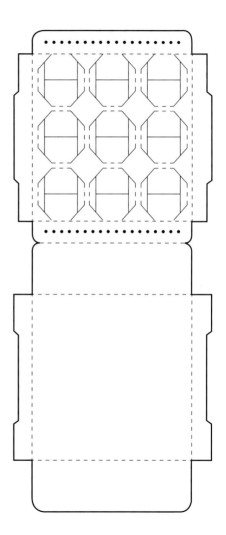

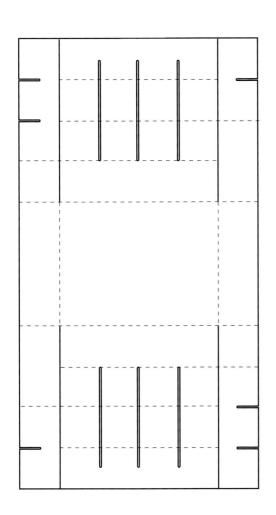

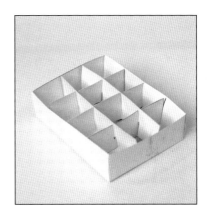

Divided Counter Display   411

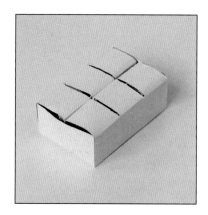

412   Divided Counter Display

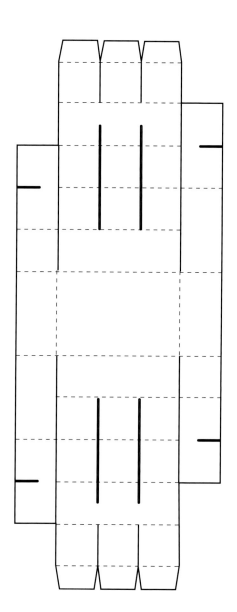

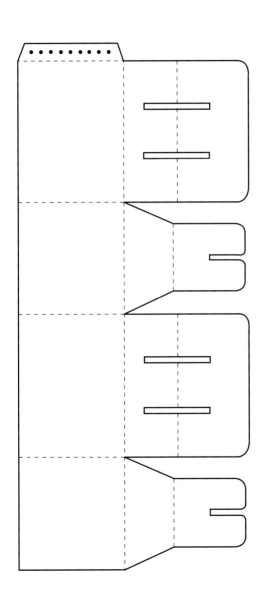

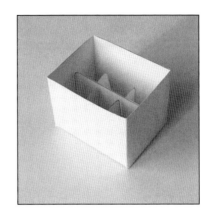

Divider Counter Display 413

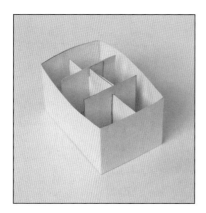

414 6-cell Auto Lock Bottom

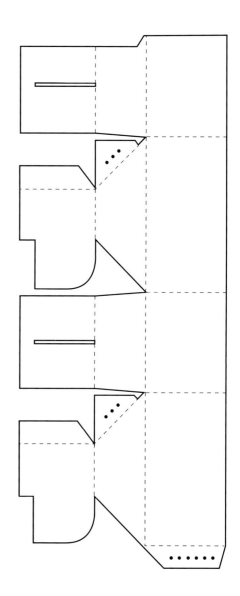

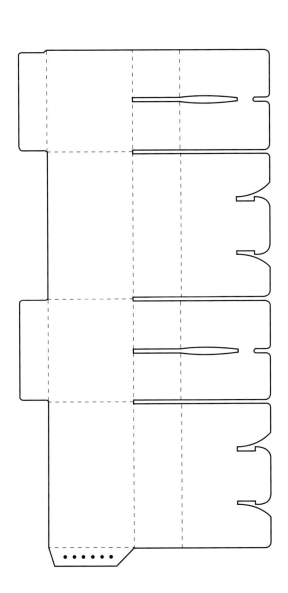

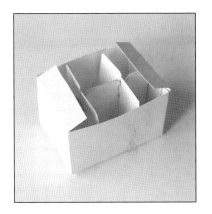

6-cell Auto Lock Bottom   415

12-cell Container

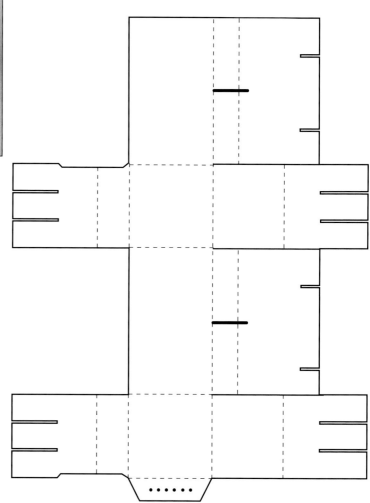

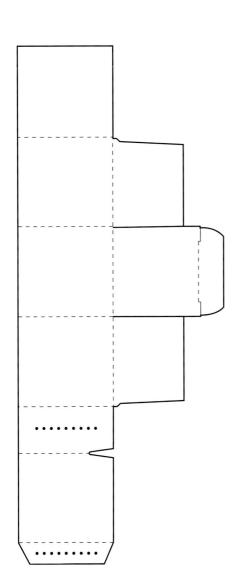

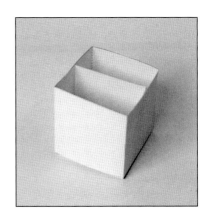

R.T.E. Lining Box 417

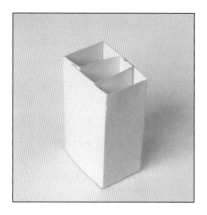

418 R.T.E. Lining Box

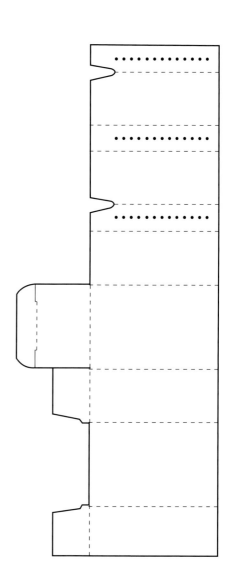

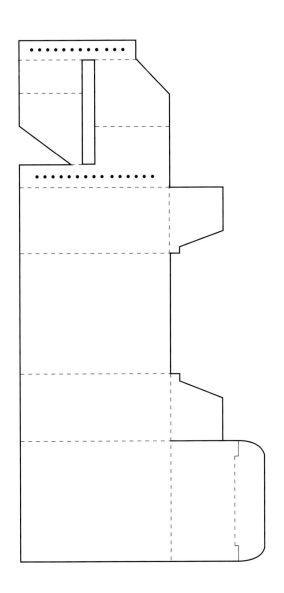

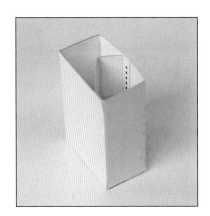

R.T.E. Lining Box   419

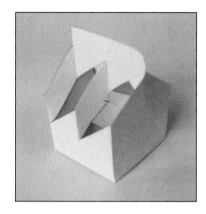

Divided Display Container

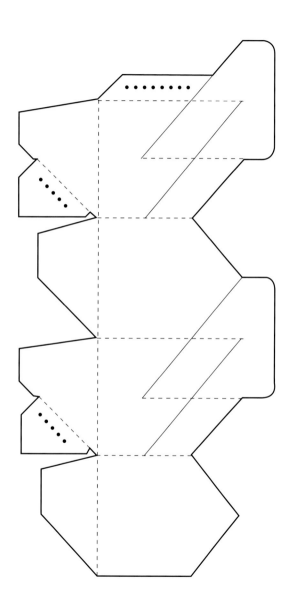

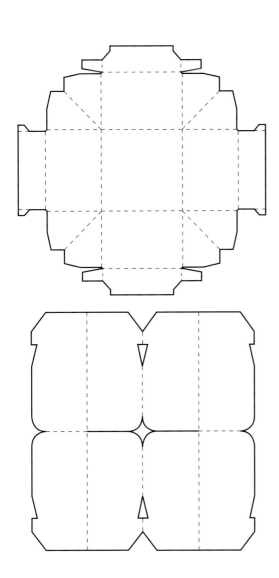

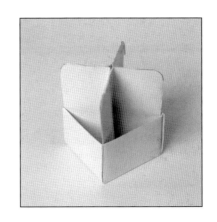

Divided Display Box 421

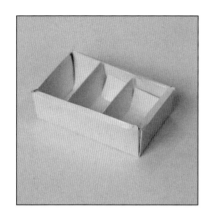

422   Divided Display Box

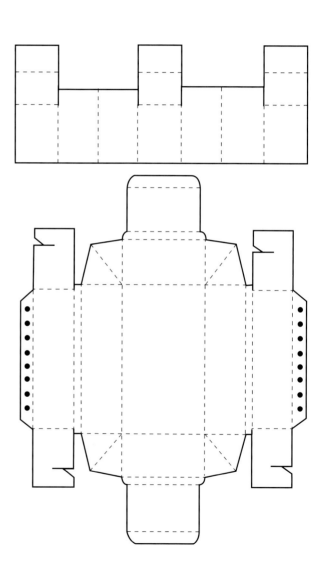

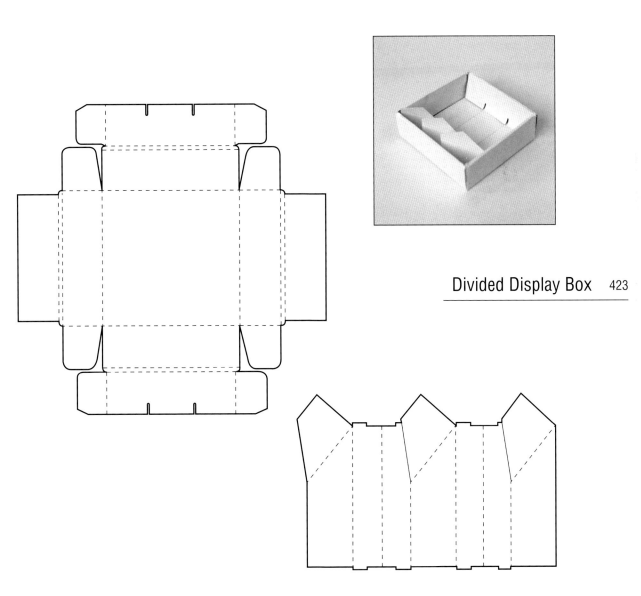

Divided Display Box 423

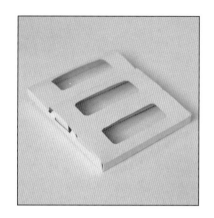

424 Divided Display Box

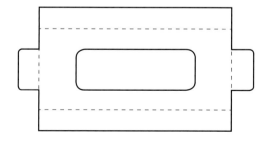

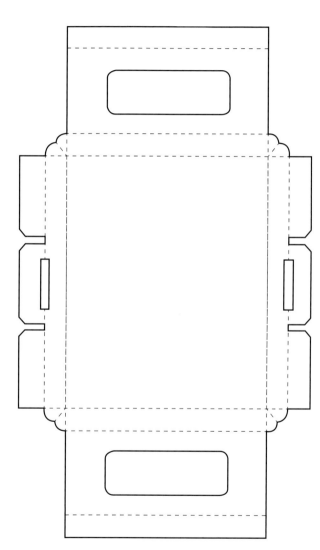

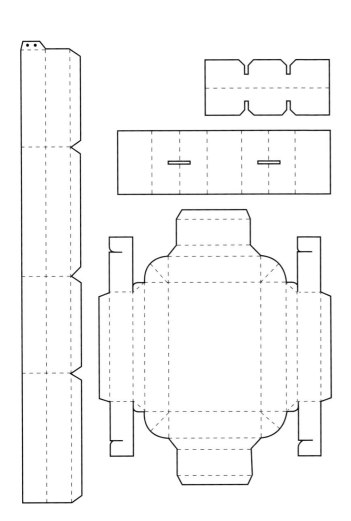

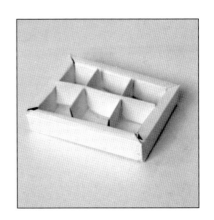

Divided Display Box 425

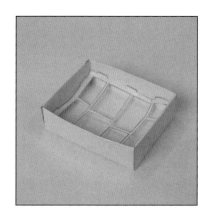

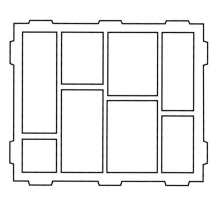

426 Divided Display Box

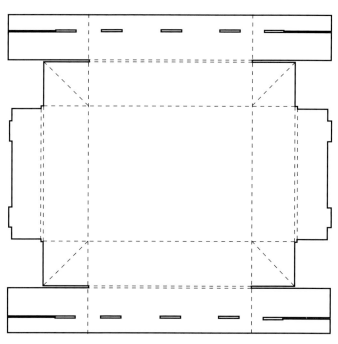

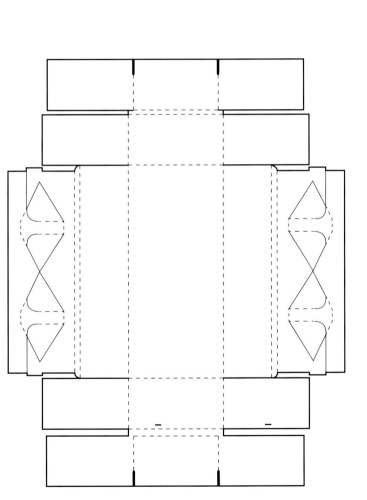

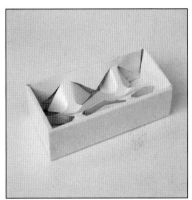

Divided Display Container 427

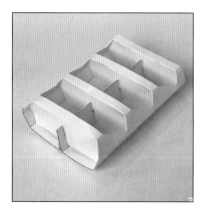

Divided Display Container

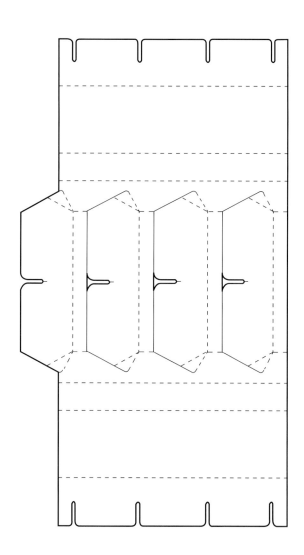

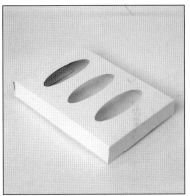

Divided Display Container   429

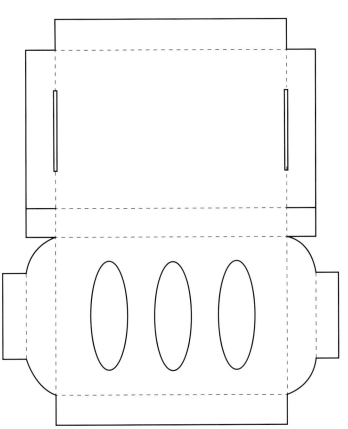

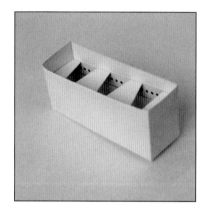

430   Divided Display Container

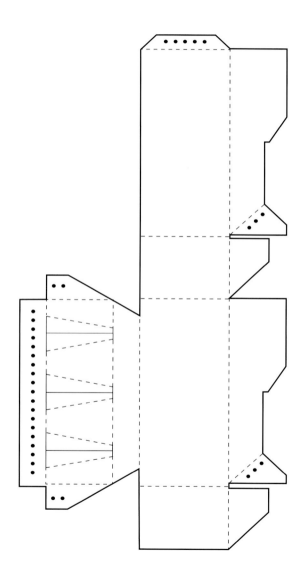

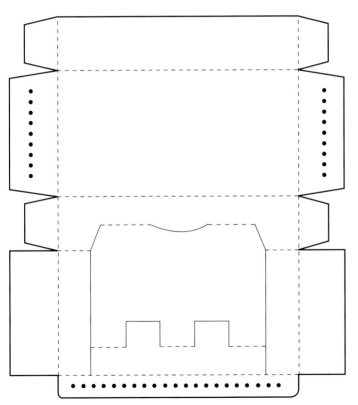

Divided Display Container   431

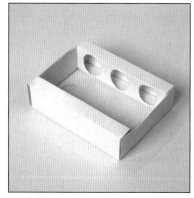

432   Divided Display Container

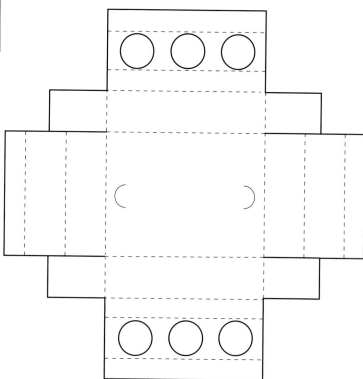

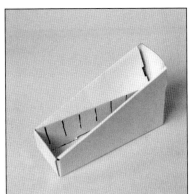

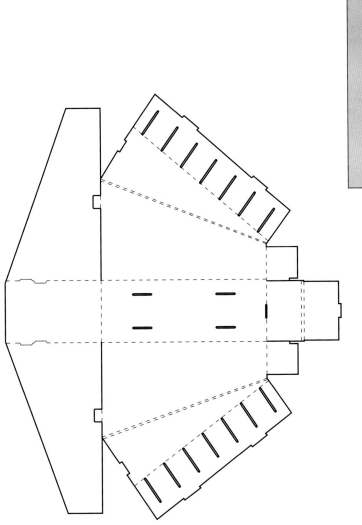

Card Display Box   433

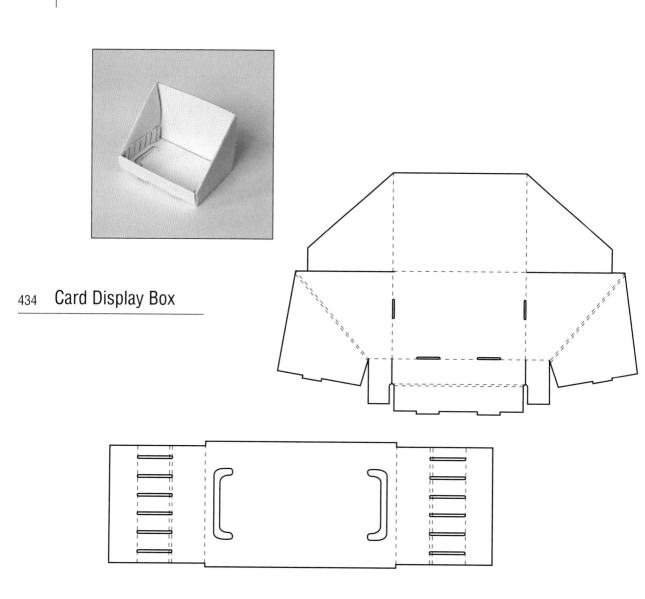

434 Card Display Box

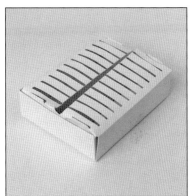

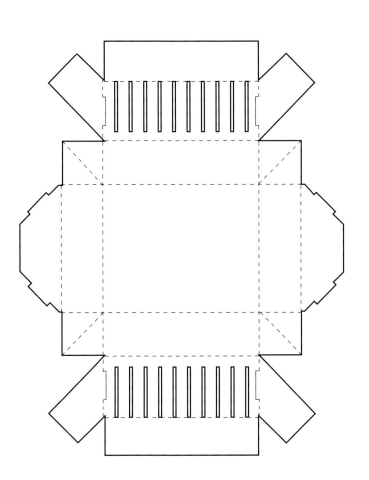

Card Display Box   435

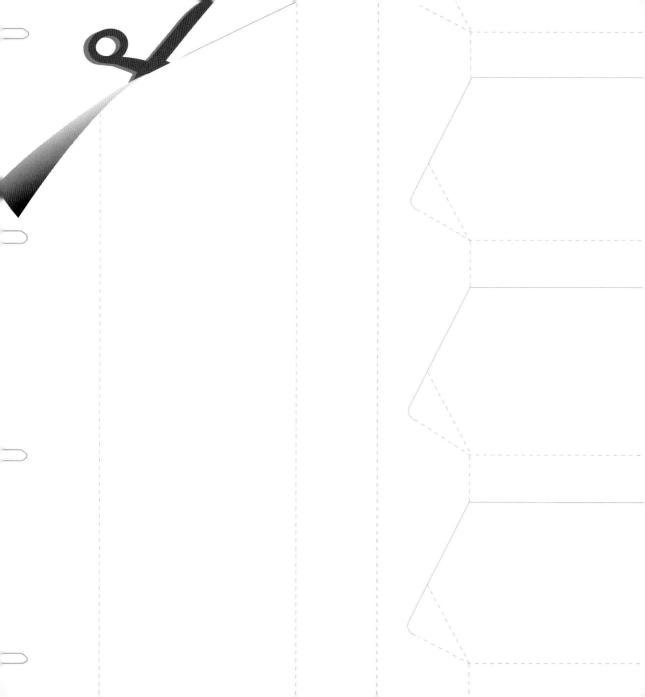

Special Shapes

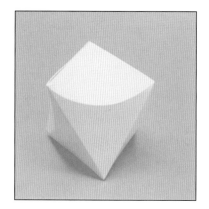

438　Diamond Box

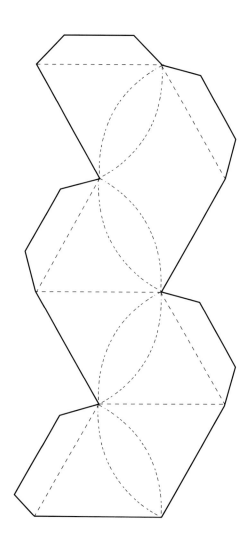

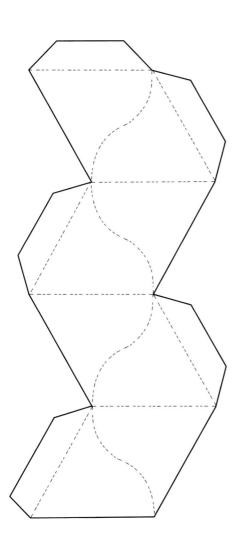

Diamond Box 439

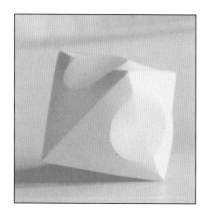

440   Diamond Box

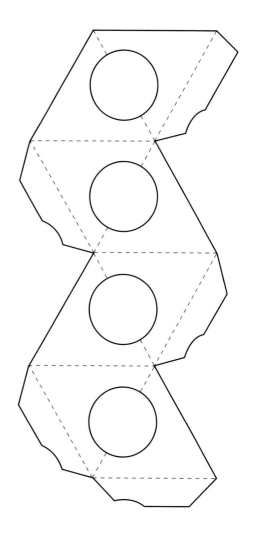

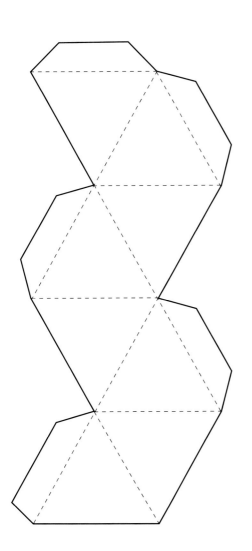

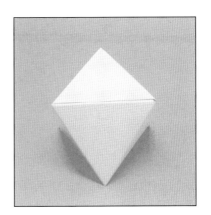

Diamond Box 441

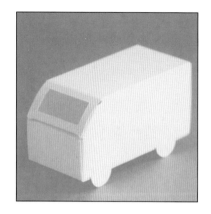

442 **Buggy Box**

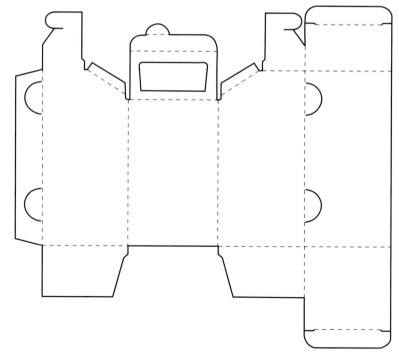

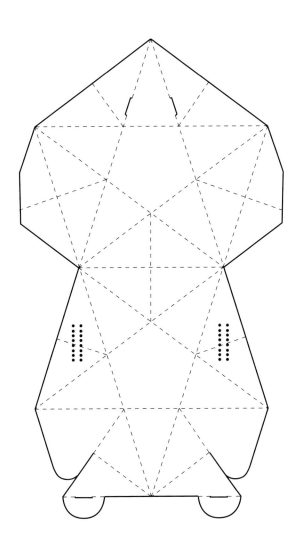

Pentagram Box 443

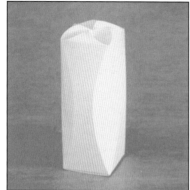

444 Box with Floral Top and Body

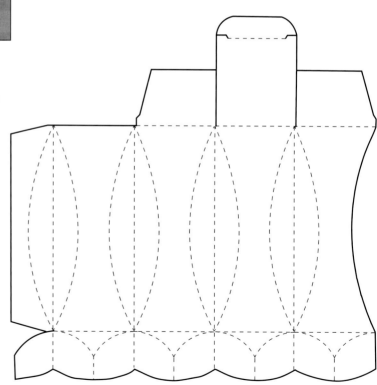

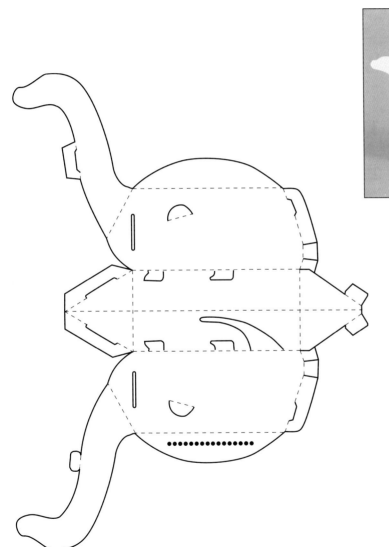

Dinosaur Box 445

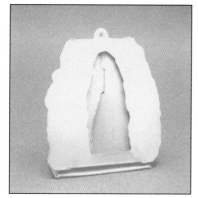

446   Perfume Box

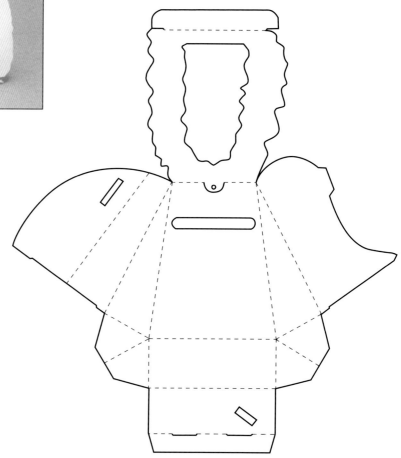

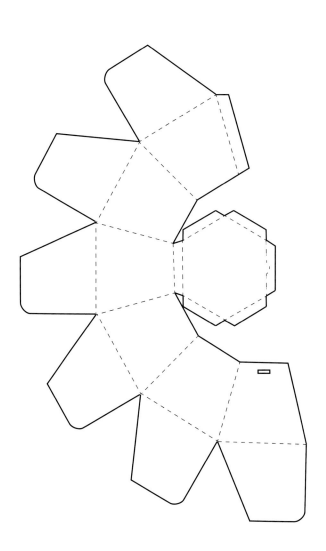

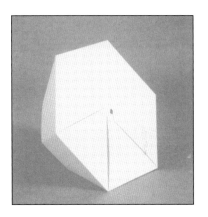

Inclined Hexagonal Box   447

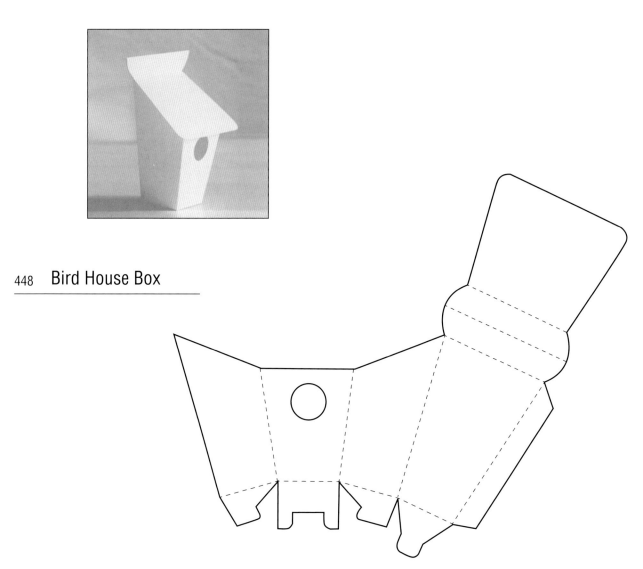

448 Bird House Box

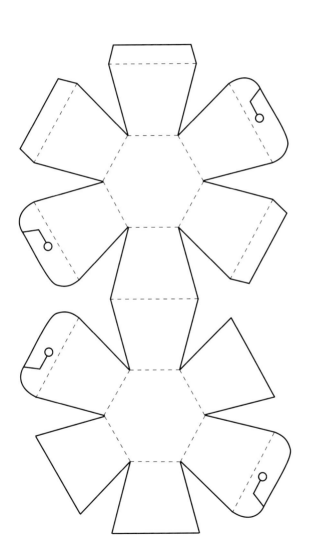

Hexagonal Jumped Box   449

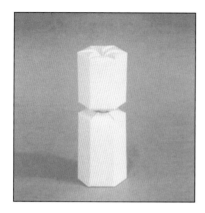

450 Hexagonal Box

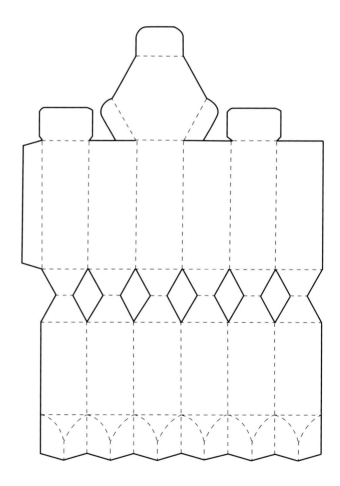

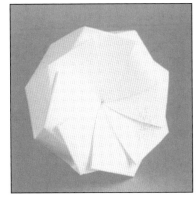

Octagonal Gift Box 451

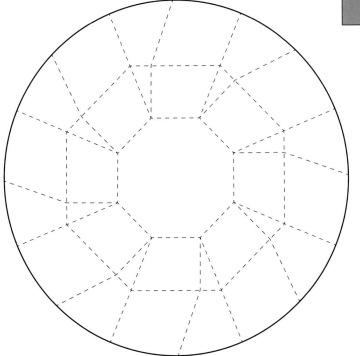

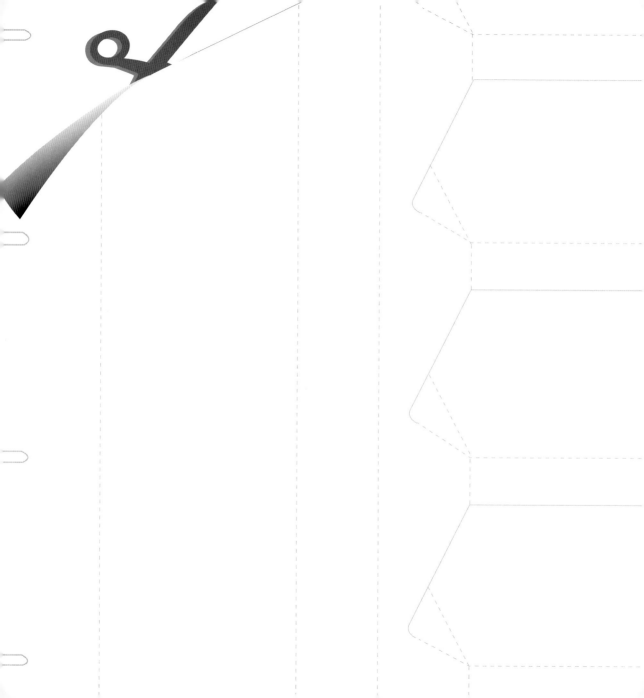

Carriers

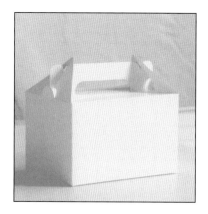

454 Double-eared Carrier

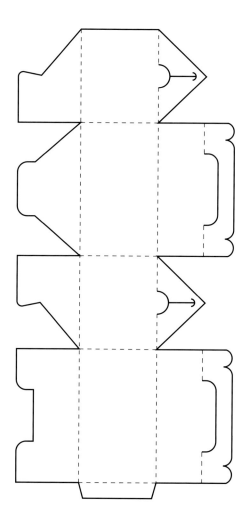

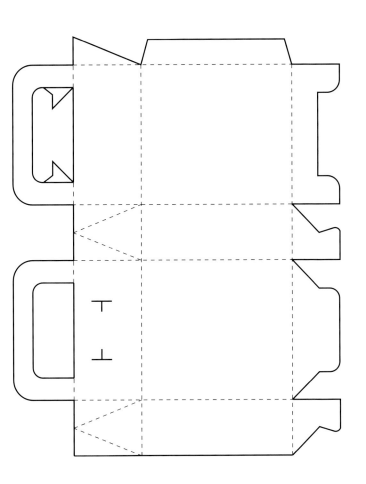

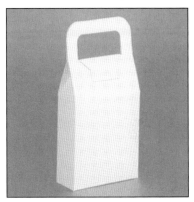

Carrier with Roof-shaped Top 455

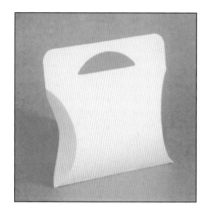

456 **Pillow Pack Carrier**

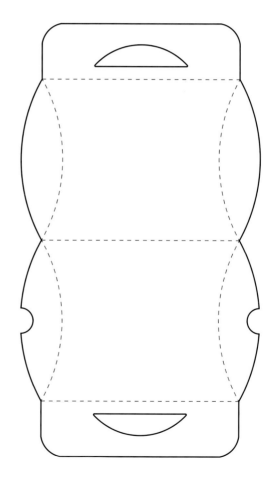

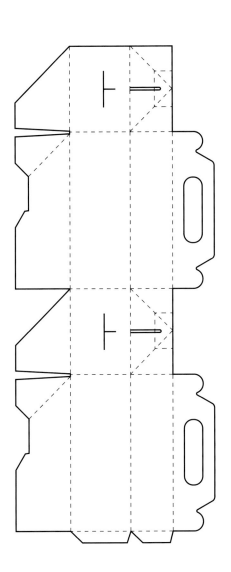

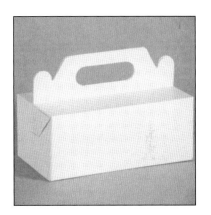

Folding Carrier 457

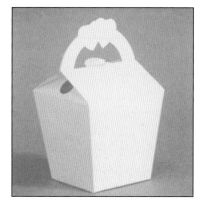

458   Gift Carrier

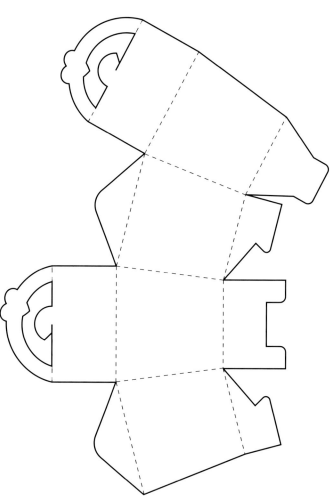

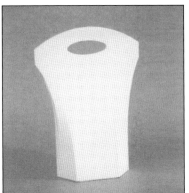

Hexagonal Carrier 459

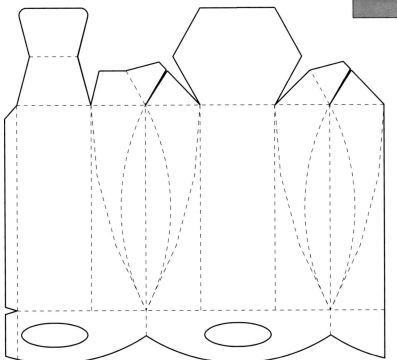

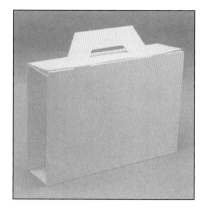

460   Carrier

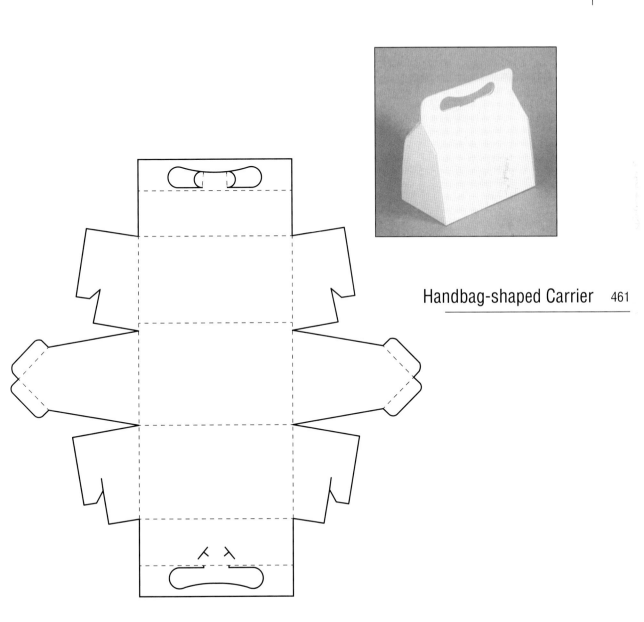

Handbag-shaped Carrier 461

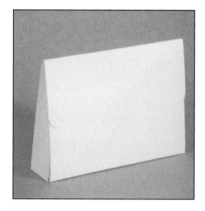

462   Purse with 123 Bottom

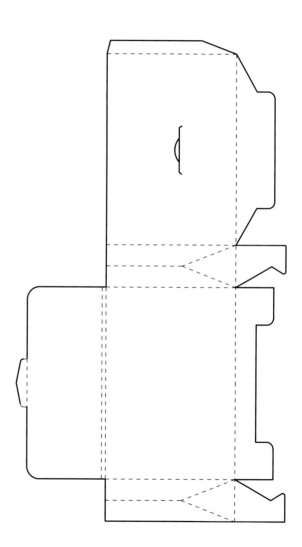

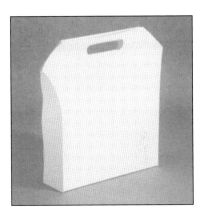

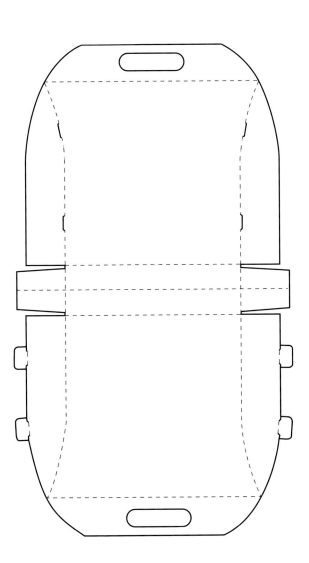

Folding Carrier 463

Gift Packaging

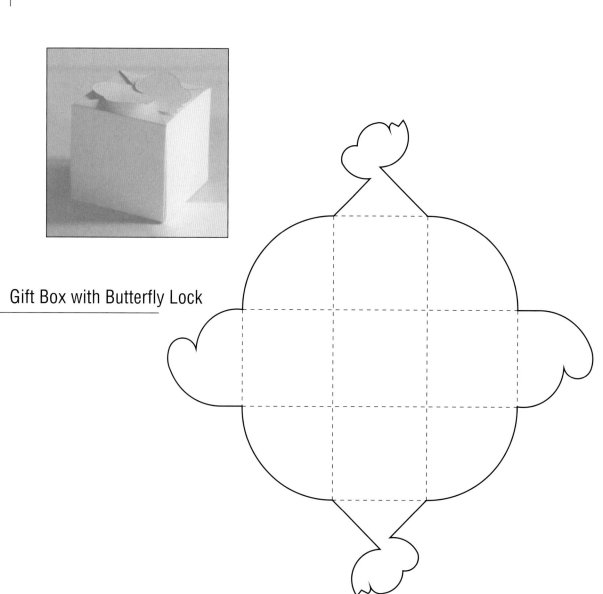

466   Gift Box with Butterfly Lock

Tall Gift Box 467

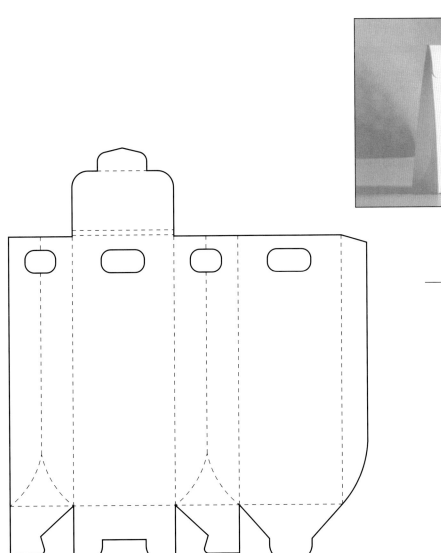

468   Gift Box with Spire and Auto Bottom

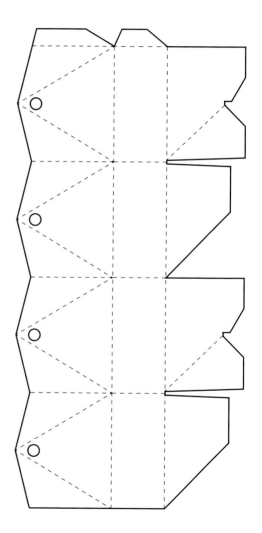

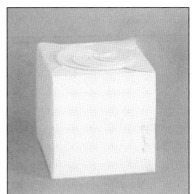

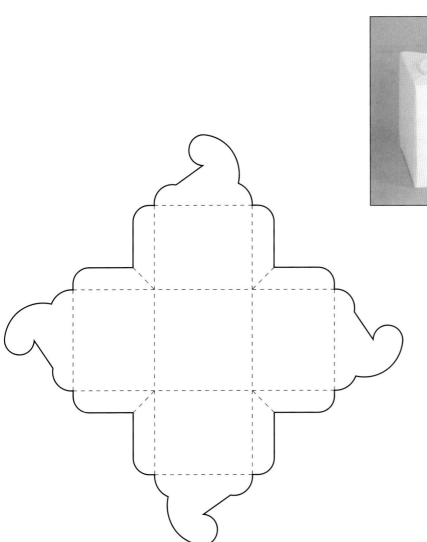

Gift Box   469

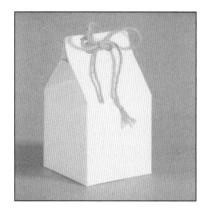

470 **Gift Box**

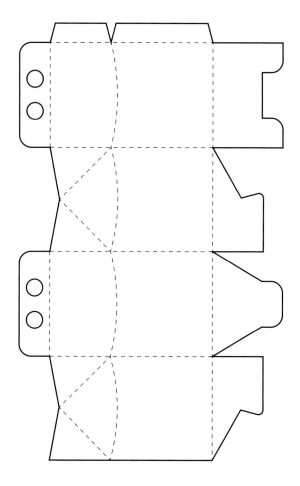

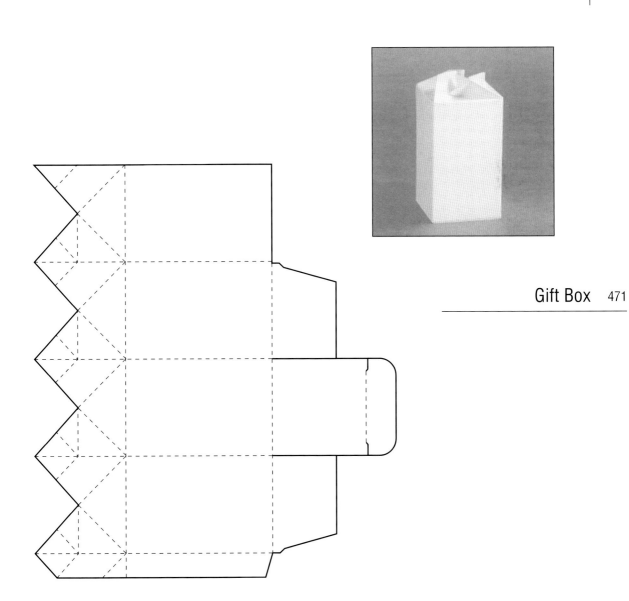

Gift Box 471

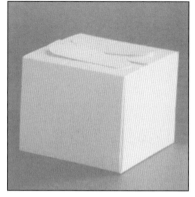

472 **Gift Box**

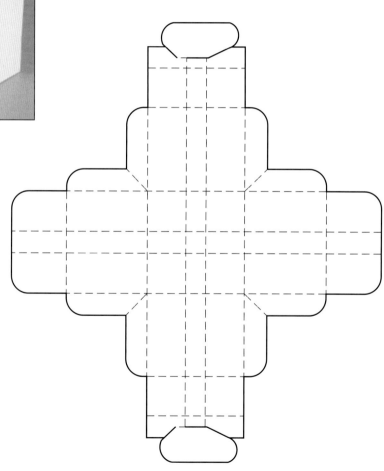

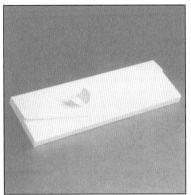

Flat Box with Lock   473

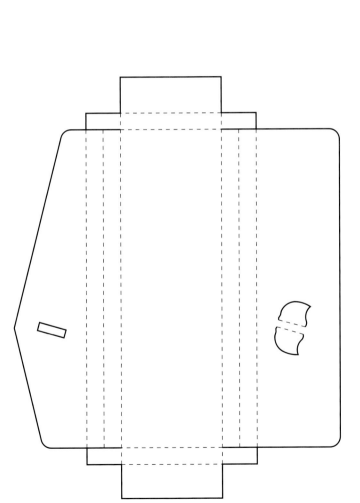

474 Gift Box

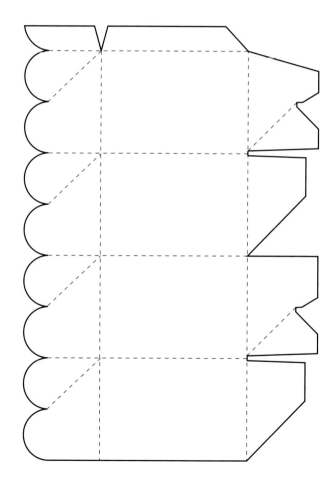

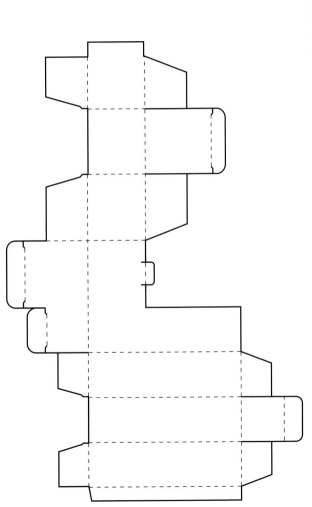

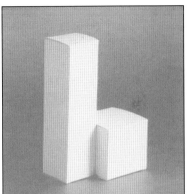

Son and Mother Box   475

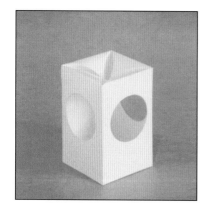

476   Gift Box

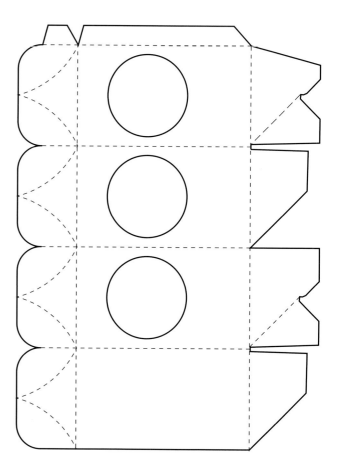

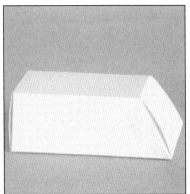

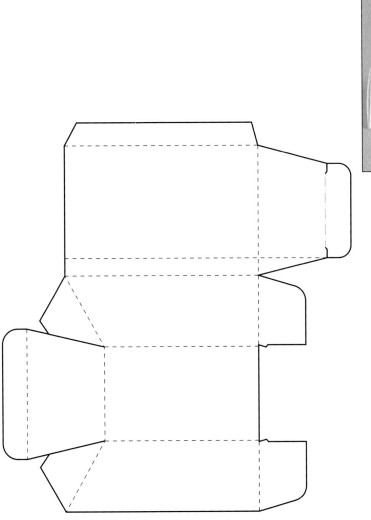

Asymmetrical Gift Box 477

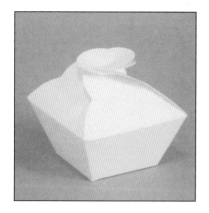

478 Inclined Gift Box with Floral Lock

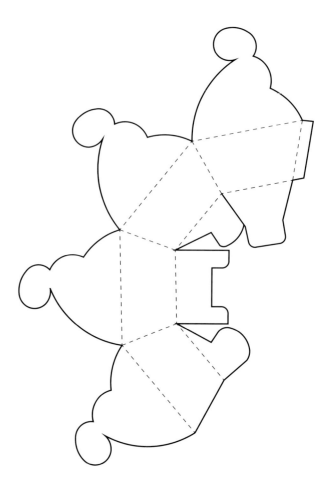

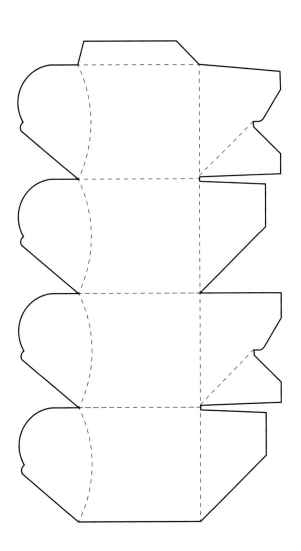

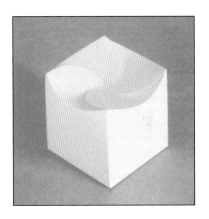

Gift Box with Floral Lock 479

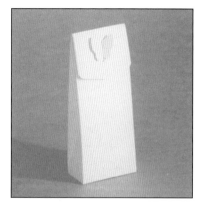

480 Gift Box with Butterfly Lock

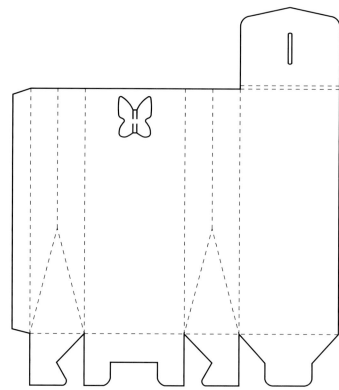

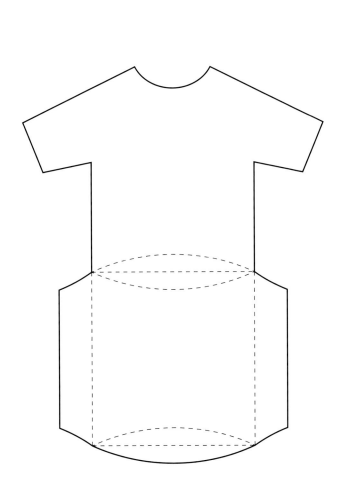

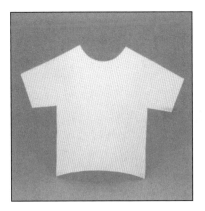

Shirt-shaped Pillow Box   481

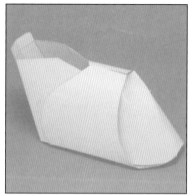

Shoe-shaped Box with Lock

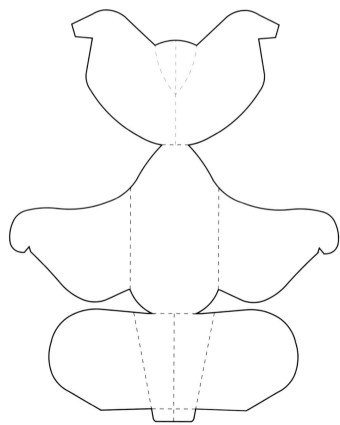

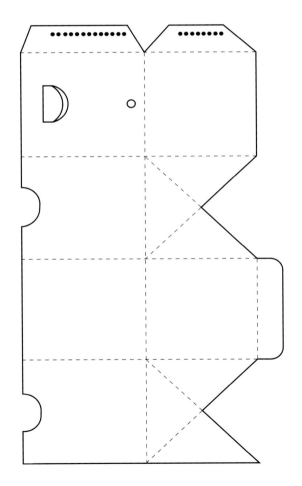

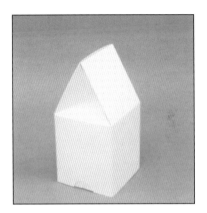

House-shaped Calendar:Top Portion   483

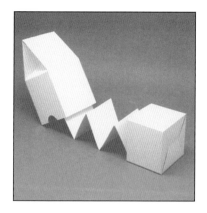

484 House-shaped Calendar:Bottom Portion

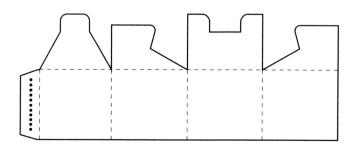

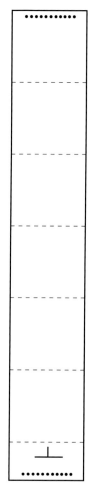

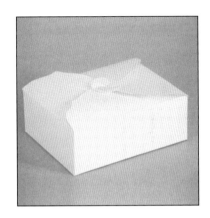

Oblong Box with Floral Lock 485

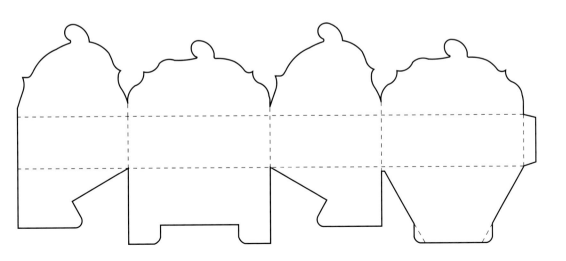

Stands

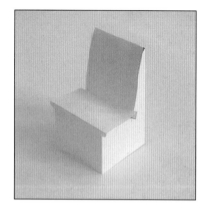

488 Display Stand

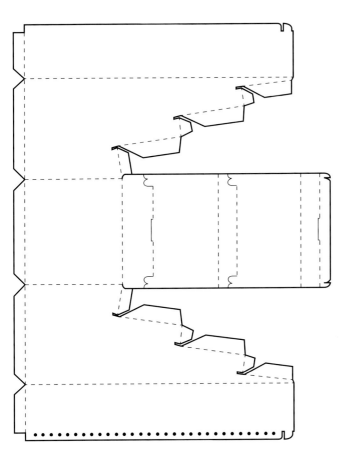

Display Stand   489

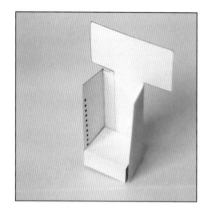

Display Stand

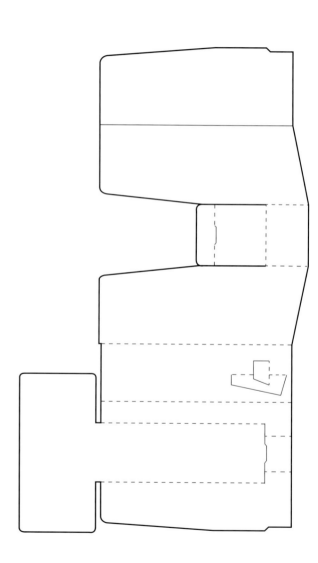

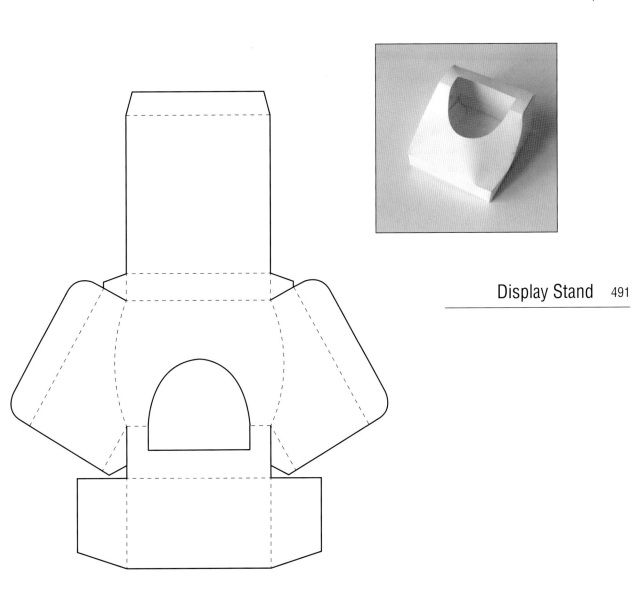

Display Stand 491

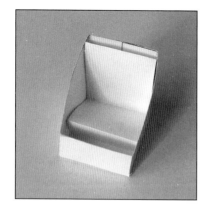

492 Display Stand

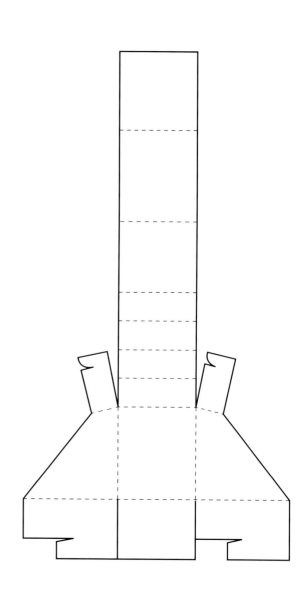

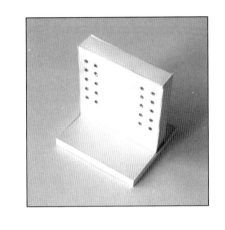

Display Stand 493

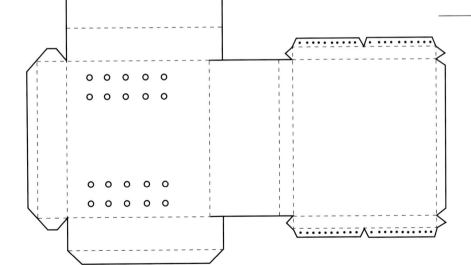

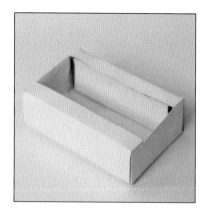

494 Display Stand

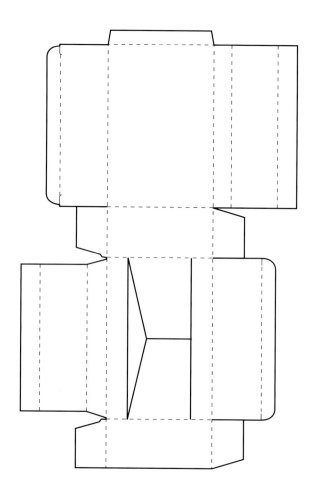

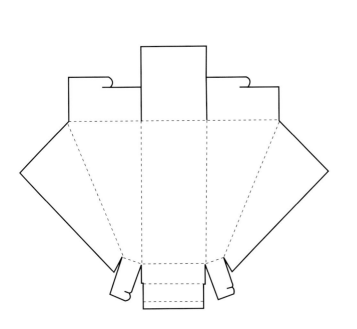

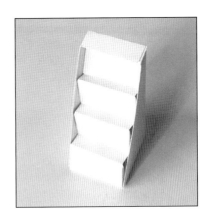

Display Stand 495

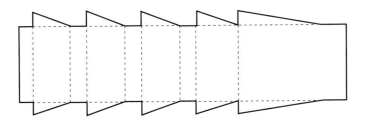

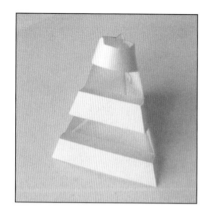

496 Display Stand

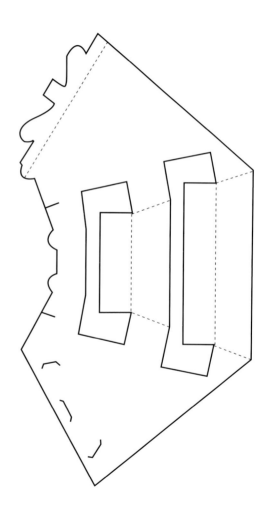

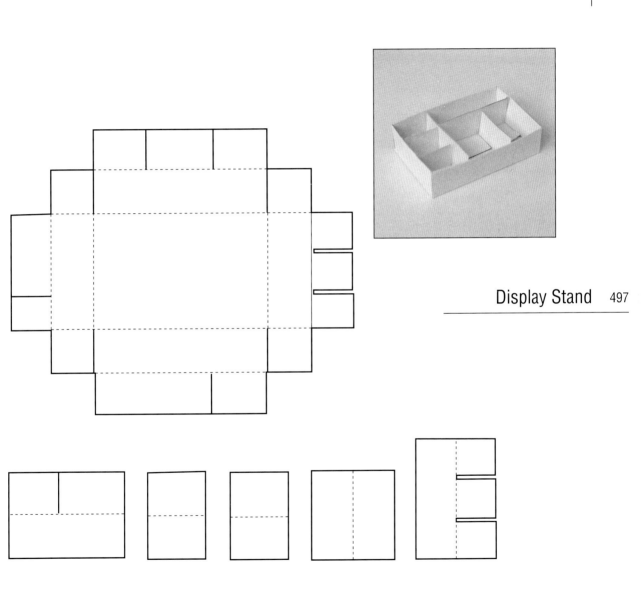

Display Stand 497

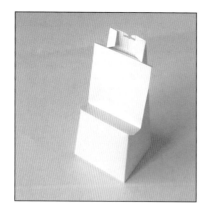

Display Stand

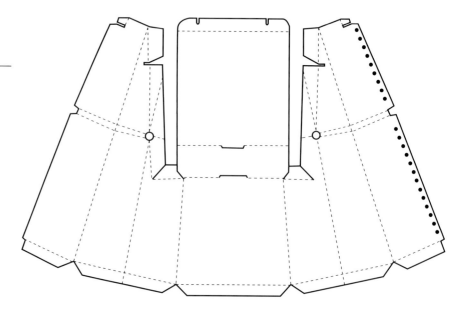

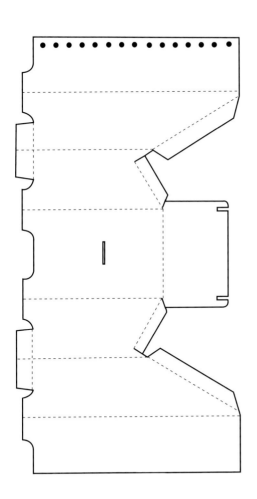

Display Stand 499

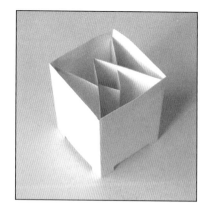

500   Display Stand

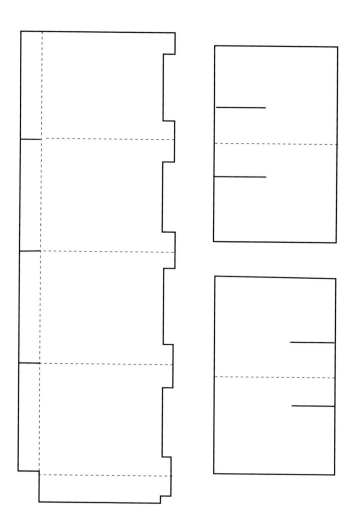

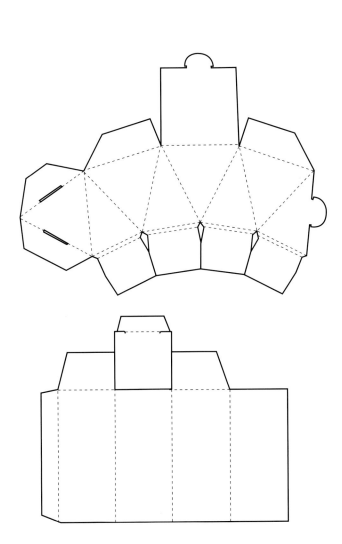

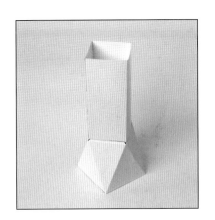

Display Stand 501

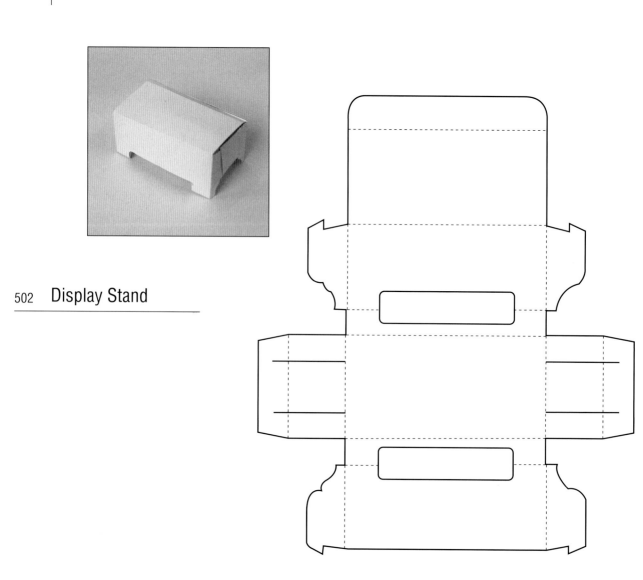

502 Display Stand

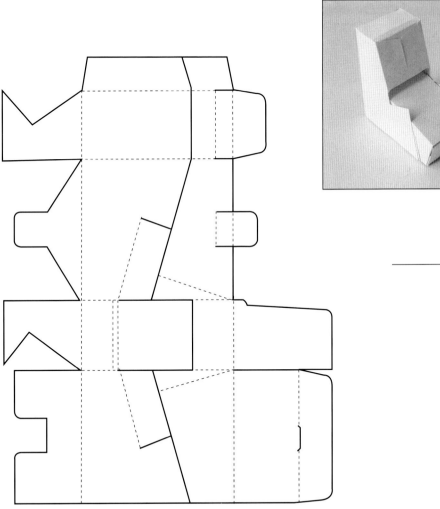

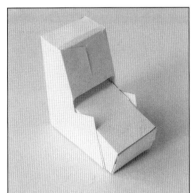

Display Stand   503

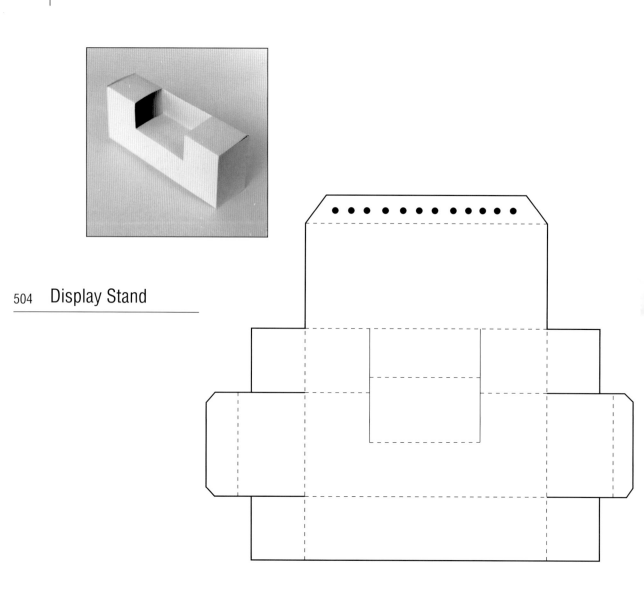

Display Stand

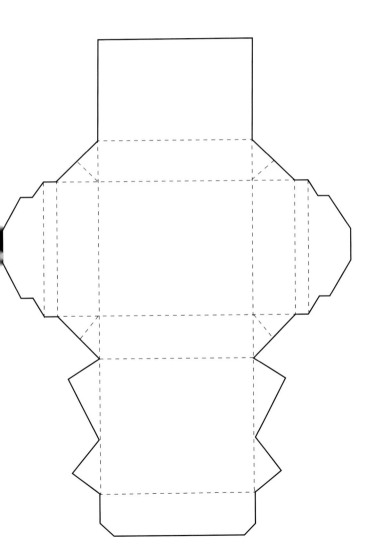

Display Stand 505

506   Display Stand

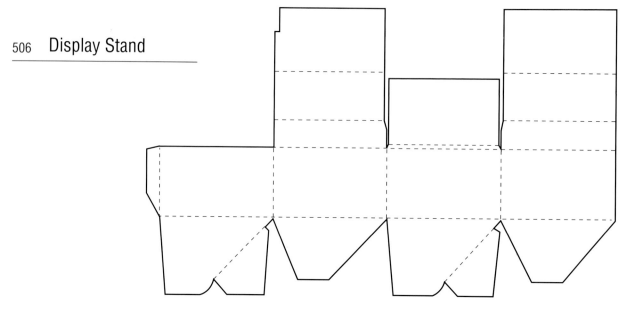

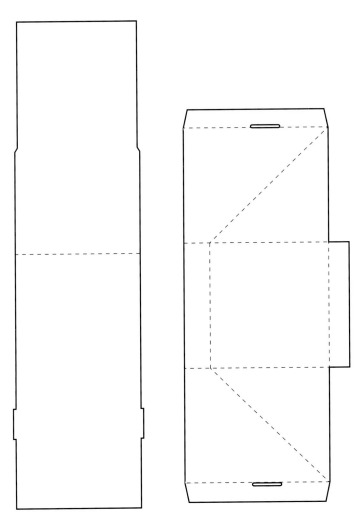

Display Stand   507

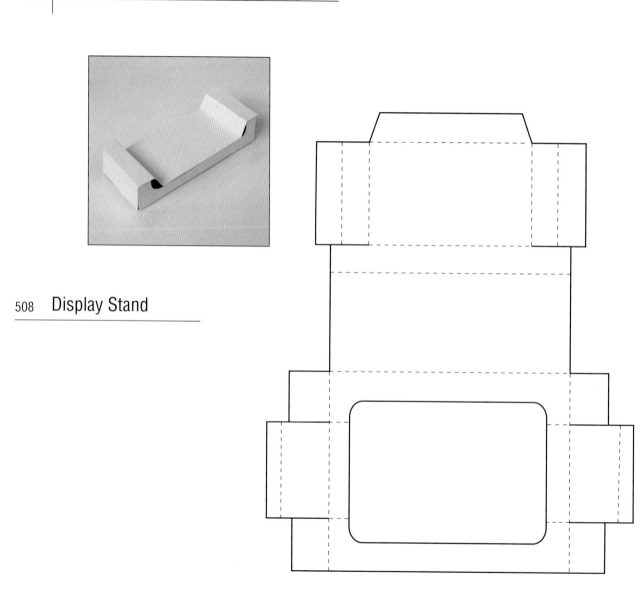

508 **Display Stand**

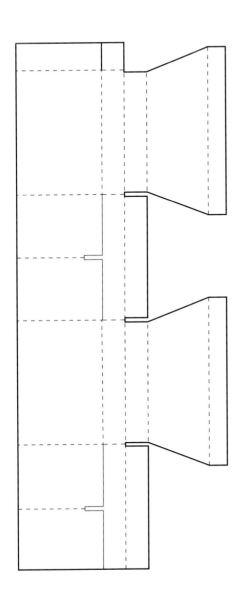

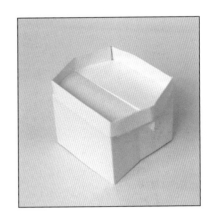

Display Stand 509

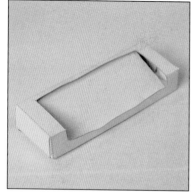

510 Display Stand

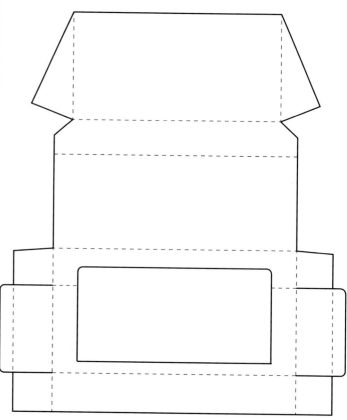

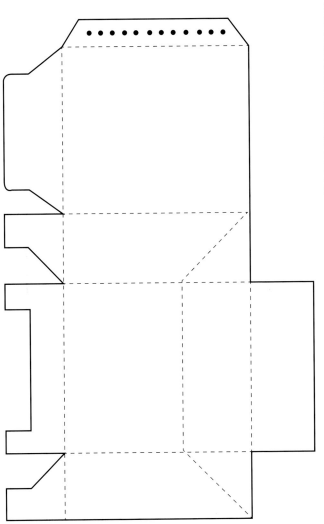

Display Stand 511

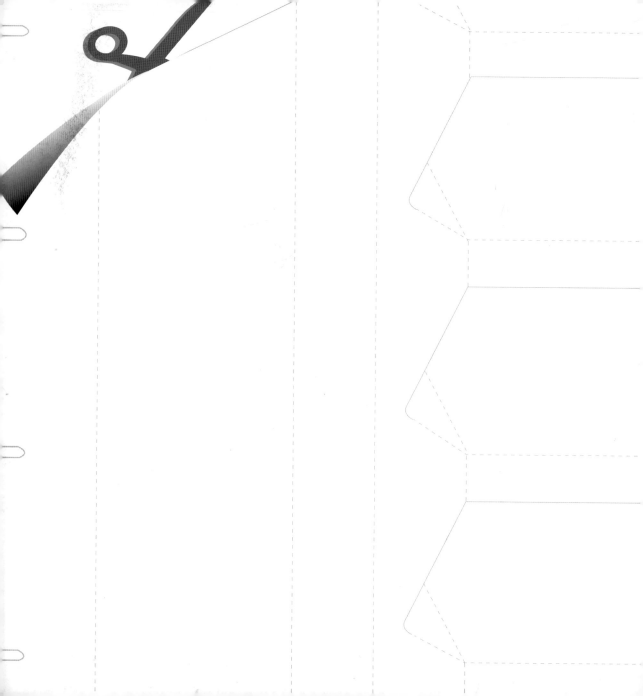